THE COMPLETE UK TOWER AIR FRYER COOKBOOK

1200 Days of Traditional and Modern British Recipes to Redefine Your Kitchen Creations | Full Colour Edition

Ellie Hartley

Copyright© 2023 By Ellie Hartley Rights Reserved

This book is copyright protected. It is only for personal use. You cannot amend, distribute, sell, use, quote or paraphrase any part of the content within this book, without the consent of the author or publisher.

Under no circumstances will any blame or legal responsibility be held against the publisher, or author, for any damages, reparation, or monetary loss due to the information contained within this book, either directly or indirectly.

Disclaimer Notice:
Please note the information contained within this document is for educational and entertainment purposes only. All effort has been executed to present accurate, up to date, reliable, complete information. No warranties of any kind are declared or implied. Readers acknowledge that the author is not engaged in the rendering of legal, financial, medical or professional advice. The content within this book has been derived from various sources. Please consult a licensed professional before attempting any techniques outlined in this book.

By reading this document, the reader agrees that under no circumstances is the author responsible for any losses, direct or indirect, that are incurred as a result of the use of the information contained within this document, including, but not limited to, errors, omissions, or inaccuracies.

Editor: LYN
Cover Art: ABR
Interior Design: A. Manikanndaprabhu
Food stylist: JO

TABLE OF CONTENTS

The Complete UK Tower Air Fryer Cookbook   1

Introduction   5

Chapter 1: Appetizers   9
- Mom's Jacket Potatoes   10
- Oyster Mushroom and Lemongrass Omelet   10
- Olive, Cheese, and Broccoli   10
- Red Cabbage and Mushroom Stickers   11
- Swiss Chard and Cheese Omelet   11
- Parmesan Cauliflower   11
- Cream Buns with Strawberries   12
- Onion Rings   12
- Spiced Nuts   13
- French Toast In Sticks   13
- Garlic Cauliflower Nuggets   13
- Chickpea & Zucchini Burgers   14
- Broccoli with Cheese & Olives   14
- Vegetable Fries   14
- Crab & Cheese Soufflé   14
- Baked Tomato & Egg   15
- Spicy Mozzarella Stick   15
- Air-Fried Walnuts & Green Beans   16
- Air-Fried Banana Turmeric Chips   16
- Tomato Vegetable Curry   16
- Air-Fried Carrots with Lemon   17
- Potato Fries with Bean Sprouts & Peanut Herb Salad   17

Chapter 2: Breakfasts   18
- Best-Ever Egg Muffins   19
- Zucchini Quiche with Sweet Potato "Crust"   19
- Cheesy Frittata   19
- Oatmeal with Strawberries   20
- Keto Breakfast Bacon   20
- Buckwheat Crepes   20
- Sausage Biscuit   21
- Homemade Granola   21
- Breakfast Pizza   21
- All Berries Pancakes   22
- Low-Carb White Egg and Spinach Frittata   22
- Pumpkin Pie French Toast   22
- Baked Mini Quiche   23
- Breakfast Chicken Hash   23
- Eggs and Cocotte On Toast   23
- Strawberries Oatmeal   24
- Bagels   24
- Breakfast Hash   25
- No-Bun Breakfast Bacon Burger   25
- Breakfast Sugar-Free Maple Cinnamon Buns   25

- Quinoa-Chicken Meatballs with Garlicky Zucchini Spirals   26

Chapter 3: Poultry   27
- Chicken and Broccoli   28
- Chicken Casserole   28
- Balsamic Chicken Roast   28
- Buttermilk Fried Chicken   29
- Turkey Croquettes   29
- Mini Turkey Meatballs   30
- Herbed Chicken Marsala   30
- Turkey and Cream Cheese Breast Pillows   31
- Chicken Tikka Kebab   31
- Soy Chicken and Sesame   32
- Bacon Chicken Breast   32
- Creamy Chicken Thighs   32
- Turkey & Cheese Calzone   33
- Ranch Chicken Wings   33
- Mozzarella Turkey Rolls   34
- Chicken Kebabs   34

Chapter 4: Beef, Pork and Lamb   35
- Mustard Pork Tenderloin   36
- Dumplings with Pork   36
- Spiced Pork Medallions   36
- Chinese Steak and Broccoli   37
- Stuffed Pork Chops   37
- Beef Wellington Wontons   37
- Beef Strips with Snow Peas and Mushrooms   38
- Beef Fillets with Garlic Mayo   38
- Chili Beef Jerky   39
- Pork Burgers with Red Cabbage Slaw   39
- Pork Trinoza Wrapped In Ham   39
- Stuffed Cabbage and Pork Loin Rolls   40
- Homemade Flamingos   40
- Pork Chops   40
- Meatballs with Sauce   41
- Crumbed Pork & Semi-Dried Tomato Pesto   41
- Chinese-Style Beef & Broccoli   42
- Diet Boiled Ribs   42

Chapter 5: Fish & Seafood   43
- Coconut Shrimp   44
- Grilled Lemon to Glazed Salmon   44
- Chipotle Spiced Shrimp   44
- Fish and Chips   44
- Sesame Salmon Kebabs with Almond Green Beans   45
- Cod Fillet   45
- Parmesan Walnut Salmon   46

Lemony and Spicy Coconut Crusted Salmon	46
Shrimp Scampi	47
Crab Cakes	47
Creamy Shrimp Nachos	47
Peppery and Lemony Haddock	48
Black Cod with Grapes, Pecans, Fennel & Kale	48
Sweet Mustard Coconut Shrimp	48
Crunchy Fish Taco	49
Grilled Salmon Fillets	49

Chapter 6: Side Dishes and Snacks — 50

Chips with Garlic and Kale	51
Balls of Salmon and Garlic	51
Stew with Mushrooms	51
Crispy Beans	51
Air Fryer Zucchini Chips	52
Mini-Meatballs	52
Bacon Wrapped Avocado Wedges	53
Herb and Lemon Cauliflower	53
Breaded Summer Squash	53
Chewy Date Bars	54
Garlic-Rosemary Brussels Sprouts	54
Kale & Celery Crackers	54
Crispy Brussels Sprouts	55
Sweet Potato Cauliflower Patties	55

Chapter 7: Vegan & Vegetarian — 56

Black Bean Burgers with Lettuce "Buns"	57
Artichokes and Hot Tomatoes with Penne	57
Fennel Braised	57
Vegetarian Chilli with Tofu	58
Sriracha Golden Cauliflower	58
Rosemary Au Gratin Potatoes	59
Chickpeas & Spinach with Coconut	59
Lemony Falafel	59
Cauliflower Rice	60
Creamed Spinach	60
American-Style Brussels Sprout Salad	61
Carrot & Zucchini Muffins	61
Carrot and Oat Balls	61

Chapter 8: Desserts — 62

Caramelized Cinnamon Peaches with Nutty Vanilla Ricotta	63
Crustless Cheesecake	63
Coconut Orange Cake	63
Fudge Brownies	64
Date & Hazelnut Cookies	64
Bread Pudding with Vanilla	64
Coconut Pie	65
Apple Pie Roll	65
Chewy White Chocolate Cookies	66
Black Bean Brownie	66
Bread Pudding with Sultanas	66
Churros	67
Air-Fryer Scones	67

Appendix 1 — 68

Appendix 2 — 69

Appendix 3 — 70

INTRODUCTION

In today's fast-paced world, where health-consciousness and busy schedules often collide, finding a cooking method that strikes a harmonious balance between convenience, health, and deliciousness can be a culinary revelation. Enter the air fryer—an innovative kitchen appliance that has taken the culinary world by storm. In this UK Tower Air Fryer Cookbook, we embark on a flavorful journey, exploring the versatility and potential of your Tower air fryer while unraveling the delectable recipes that await you. This introduction serves as your guide to not only understanding the essence of air frying but also comprehending what this cookbook has in store for you and how to utilize it effectively.

The Essence of Air Frying

Before delving into the heart of this cookbook, it's essential to grasp the fundamental concept of air frying. At its core, an air fryer is a compact yet powerful countertop appliance that relies on hot air circulation to cook food to crispy perfection. Unlike traditional deep frying, which submerges food in a pool of oil, air frying uses minimal to no oil, making it a healthier alternative without compromising on taste or texture.

Healthier Cooking Revolutionized: One of the most remarkable aspects of air frying is its ability to transform how we approach cooking. Traditional frying methods involve submerging food in a bath of hot oil, resulting in dishes that are not only calorie-dense but also laden with unhealthy fats. Air frying, on the other hand, accomplishes the same crispy texture and delicious flavor without the need for excessive oil. This revolutionary approach significantly reduces the calorie content of your favorite fried foods, making them more waistline-friendly while preserving their taste.

Hot Air Circulation: The secret behind the magic of air frying lies in the way it circulates hot air. The Tower Air Fryer, a true hero in your kitchen, exemplifies this concept beautifully. This countertop dynamo is equipped with a powerful fan that swiftly and evenly distributes hot air around the food. This consistent air circulation ensures that every nook and cranny of your culinary creations is exposed to the ideal cooking temperature. Whether you're air frying a batch of crispy chicken wings, roasting vegetables, or baking delicate pastries, the Tower Air Fryer ensures that each dish emerges with a satisfying crunch and mouthwatering flavor.

Precision Temperature Control: The Tower Air Fryer is not just an appliance; it's your culinary partner in precision. Its intuitive controls allow you to set precise temperatures, ensuring that your dishes are cooked to perfection. From low-and-slow cooking for tender meats to high-temperature blasts for creating that coveted golden crust, this air fryer offers a wide range of cooking possibilities at your fingertips.

Minimal Oil, Maximum Flavor: The concept of air frying hinges on the minimal use of oil, and the Tower Air Fryer exemplifies this principle. While traditional frying methods require quarts of oil to submerge your ingredients completely, air frying often needs just a fraction of that. This means that your dishes are less greasy and heavy, allowing the natural flavors of your ingredients to shine through. You'll find that your taste buds are treated to a heightened sensation of each ingredient's inherent taste, making your culinary creations not only healthier but also more delicious.

Unveiling the Culinary Treasures within

This cookbook is more than just a compilation of recipes; it's a treasure trove of carefully curated culinary creations waiting to be discovered. We've meticulously selected each recipe, thoughtfully designing them to cater to a vast array of tastes and dietary preferences. From tantalizing starters that set the tone for your meal to hearty mains that steal the spotlight, from delightful sides that elevate any dish to irresistible desserts that provide the perfect sweet finale—our collection has been crafted with your gastronomic desires in mind.

A Journey Through Culinary Diversity: The pages of this cookbook are a culinary adventure, taking you on a journey through diverse cuisines, flavors, and ingredients. We've ventured far and wide to bring you a rich tapestry of recipes inspired by global culinary traditions. From the comforting embrace of classic comfort foods to the exotic allure of international fare, our cookbook reflects the diverse and ever-evolving palate of the modern food lover. Each recipe is a passport to a new culinary destination, inviting you to explore the world's flavors from the comfort of your kitchen.

Accessible to All: Whether you're a novice cook taking your first steps in the culinary world or a seasoned pro seeking fresh inspiration, our collection of recipes is tailored to accommodate all skill levels. We understand that everyone has to start somewhere, and we've designed this cookbook to be your trusty guide. Novices will appreciate the straightforward instructions and helpful tips, while experienced cooks will find ample room for creativity and experimentation. Cooking should be an enjoyable experience for all, and this cookbook aims to make that a reality.

Dietary Delights: We recognize that dietary preferences and requirements vary widely. Inclusivity is at the heart of our cookbook, and we've gone to great lengths to provide options for everyone. Whether you follow a vegetarian, vegan, or keto diet, or if you're simply looking for lighter, healthier meal choices, you'll find recipes that cater to your specific needs. Our goal is to empower you to make choices that align with your lifestyle while savoring every bite.

A Culinary Education: Beyond providing recipes, this cookbook is also a valuable source of culinary education. Each recipe is an opportunity to learn new techniques, discover ingredient pairings, and understand the art of balancing flavors. You'll find tips and tricks throughout the book that not only guide you through the recipes but also enhance your overall cooking skills. It's a culinary journey that encourages growth and exploration in the kitchen.

How to Use This Book

Navigating the UK Tower Air Fryer Cookbook is designed to be as straightforward as possible, ensuring that your culinary adventure with your Tower air fryer is both enjoyable and satisfying. Here's a brief guide on how to make the most of this cookbook:

1. **Introduction**: Begin by reading this introduction to gain a comprehensive understanding of air frying, the essence of the Tower Air Fryer, and the culinary treasures that lie ahead.
2. **Familiarize Yourself with Your Air Fryer**: Before diving into the recipes, take a moment to acquaint yourself with your Tower Air Fryer. Ensure it's clean, and read its manual to understand its features, controls, and safety precautions.
3. **Recipe Selection**: Peruse the cookbook and select a recipe that piques your interest or suits your dietary needs. Each recipe is accompanied by a clear title, ingredients, and step-by-step instructions.
4. **Ingredients and Equipment**: Check that you have all the required ingredients and equipment on hand. Be creative with ingredient substitutions if necessary, and ensure your Tower Air Fryer is ready for action.
5. **Follow the Instructions**: Follow the recipe instructions carefully, paying attention to cooking times and temperatures. Utilize the precise temperature control of your air fryer for optimal results.
6. **Experiment and Customize**: Feel free to experiment and customize recipes to your liking. Cooking is an art, and your Tower Air Fryer is a versatile canvas. Adjust seasoning, ingredients, or cooking times to suit your taste.
7. **Keep Notes**: Keep a notebook handy to jot down any modifications or personal preferences you discover during your cooking adventures. These notes will serve as valuable references for future culinary experiments.
8. **Maintenance**: After each use, ensure you clean your Tower Air Fryer according to the manufacturer's instructions. A well-maintained air fryer ensures consistent performance.
9. **Explore Variety**: Don't be afraid to explore the diverse range of recipes in this cookbook. From breakfast to dessert, and everything in between, there's a wealth of culinary experiences waiting for you to savor.
10. **Share and Enjoy**: Lastly, share your culinary creations with family and friends. Food brings people together, and your creations are meant to be enjoyed and celebrated.

Conclusion

In essence, the UK Tower Air Fryer Cookbook is your culinary companion, ready to inspire and empower you to create mouthwatering, healthier meals with ease. Whether you're seeking inspiration for a quick weeknight dinner, planning an elaborate weekend feast, or simply looking to add a touch of creativity to your cooking repertoire, this cookbook has you covered. As you embark on a flavorful journey with your Tower Air Fryer, let the recipes within these pages transform your culinary experiences and enrich your understanding of healthier cooking. Happy air frying!

Air Fryer Cooking Chart

Food	Temperature (°C)	Cooking Time (minutes)
French fries (thin)	200	10-15
French fries (thick)	200	15-20
Chicken wings	180	20-25
Chicken breast	180	15-20
Salmon fillet	200	8-10
Shrimp	200	8-10
Onion rings	200	8-10
Vegetables (broccoli, etc.)	180	10-15
Frozen vegetables (mix)	180	10-15
Breaded fish fillets	200	10-12
Hamburgers	200	8-10
Bacon	180	6-8
Sausages	180	12-15
Meatballs	180	12-15
Baked potatoes	200	45-50
Sweet potatoes	200	20-25
Chicken breasts	200	15-20 min
Chicken thighs	200	20-25 min
Chicken wings	200	18-20 min
Fish fillets	200	8-12 min
Shrimp	200	6-8 min
Scallops	200	6-8 min
Salmon	200	10-12 min
Pork chops	200	12-15 min

Food	Temperature (°C)	Cooking Time (minutes)
Pork tenderloin	200	20-25 min
Steak (1 inch thick)	200	8-10 min
Hamburger patties	200	8-10 min
Hot dogs/sausages	200	6-8 min
French fries	200	15-20 min
Sweet potato fries	200	15-20 min
Potato wedges	200	15-20 min
Onion rings	200	12-15 min
Zucchini/squash fries	200	10-12 min
Broccoli/cauliflower	200	8-10 min
Brussel sprouts	200	12-15 min
Carrots	200	12-15 min
Asparagus	200	6-8 min
Corn on the cob	200	12-15 min
Baked potatoes	200	40-45 min
Stuffed mushrooms	200	8-10 min
Roasted peppers	200	8-10 min
Chicken nuggets	200	10-12 min
Meatballs	200	10-12 min
Spring rolls	200	10-12 min
Mozzarella sticks	200	6-8 min
Jalapeno poppers	200	8-10 min
Quiche	180	25-30 min
Puff pastry	200	10-12 min
Apple turnovers	200	12-15 min
Chocolate chip cookies	180	6-8 min

Note: Cooking times may vary depending on the type and brand of air fryer, as well as the size and thickness of the food being cooked. Always refer to the manufacturer's instructions and use a food thermometer to ensure that food is cooked to a safe temperature.

CHAPTER 1:
APPETIZERS

MOM'S JACKET POTATOES

PREP TIME: 5 MINUTES | COOK TIME: 20 MINUTES | SERVES 4

- 6mg Cottage cheese, softened
- 6mg Parmigiano-Reggiano cheese, grated
- 1 teaspoon black pepper
- 1 1/2 heaping tablespoons roughly chopped cilantro leaves
- 18mg green onions, finely chopped
- 4 average-sized potatoes
- 2 1/2 tablespoons softened butter
- 1 teaspoon salt

1. Preheat your air fryer to 175°C.
2. Stab the potatoes with a fork. Cook them in the air fryer basket for 20 minutes, or until they are soft.
3. While the potatoes are cooking, make the filling by mixing together the cottage cheese, Parmesan cheese, black pepper, coriander, and spring onions.
4. When the potatoes are cooked, cut them in half lengthwise and scoop out the flesh. Mash the flesh with the butter and salt.
5. Stuff the potato skins with the mashed potato mixture and top with the remaining filling.
6. Air fry for an additional 5 minutes, or until the filling is heated through.
7. Serve immediately.

OYSTER MUSHROOM AND LEMONGRASS OMELET

PREP TIME: 7 MINUTES | COOK TIME: 35 MINUTES | SERVES 2

- 2 king oyster mushrooms, thinly sliced
- 1 lemongrass, chopped
- 5mg dried marjoram
- 2 eggs
- 1/3 cup Swiss cheese, grated
- 2 tablespoons sour cream
- 1 1/2 teaspoon dried rosemary
- 10mg red pepper flakes, crushed
- 10ml butter, melted
- 30g onion
- 1/2 teaspoon garlic powder
- 1 teaspoon dried dill weed
- Sea salt
- Ground black pepper, to your liking

1. Preheat your air fryer to 165°C.
2. Melt the butter in a skillet over medium heat. Add the onion, mushrooms, and lemongrass and cook until softened, about 5 minutes.
3. In a bowl, whisk together the eggs, sour cream, rosemary, red pepper flakes, garlic powder, marjoram, and dill. Season with salt and pepper.
4. Grease an air fryer baking dish with cooking spray. Pour in the egg mixture and top with the mushroom mixture and Gruyère cheese.
5. Air fry for 25-30 minutes, or until the frittata is set and the cheese is melted and golden brown.
6. Serve immediately.

OLIVE, CHEESE, AND BROCCOLI

PREP TIME: 7 MINUTES | COOK TIME: 15 MINUTES | SERVES 4

- 900g broccoli florets
- 4 tablespoons olive oil
- 60g Parmesan cheese, shaved
- 2 teaspoons lemon zest, grated
- 80g Kalamata olives, halved and pitted
- 1 teaspoon black pepper
- 1 teaspoon sea salt
- Water

1. Bring the water to a boil in a pan over medium heat and cook the broccoli for about 4 minutes. Drain.
2. Add the broccoli, salt, pepper, and olive oil to a bowl and toss to coat.
3. Place the broccoli in the air fryer basket and cook at 200°C/400°F for 15 minutes, stirring twice during cooking time.
4. Place the broccoli on a plate and toss with lemon zest, cheese, and olives.

RED CABBAGE AND MUSHROOM STICKERS

PREP TIME: 12 MINUTES | COOK TIME: 15 MINUTES | SERVES 4

- 225 grams red cabbage, shredded
- 50 grams button mushrooms, chopped
- 50 grams carrot, grated
- 2 tablespoons onion, minced
- 2 garlic cloves, minced
- 2 teaspoons fresh ginger, grated
- 12 gyoza wrappers
- 3 teaspoons olive oil, divided
- 1 tablespoon water

1. Preheat the air fryer to 190 degrees Celsius (375 degrees Fahrenheit).
2. Combine the red cabbage, mushrooms, carrot, onion, garlic, and ginger in a baking dish. Add 1 tablespoon of water.
3. Bake in the air fryer for 6 minutes, or until the vegetables are crisp-tender. Drain and set aside.
4. Working one at a time, place the gyoza wrappers on a work surface. Top each wrapper with a scant 1 tablespoon of the filling. Fold half of the wrapper over the other half to form a half-circle. Dab with water and press both edges together.
5. Spread 1 teaspoon of olive oil on the baking dish. Put half of the gyoza, seam-side up, in the dish. Air fry for 5 minutes. Add 1 tablespoon of water and return the dish to the air fryer.
6. Air fry for 4 minutes more, or until hot. Repeat with the remaining gyoza, the remaining 1 teaspoon of oil, and another tablespoon of water. Serve immediately.

SWISS CHARD AND CHEESE OMELET

PREP TIME: 7 MINUTES | COOK TIME: 18 MINUTES | SERVES 2

- 1 teaspoon garlic paste
- 1 1/2 tablespoons olive oil
- 120 milliliters crème fraiche
- 1/3 teaspoon ground black pepper
- 40 grams Swiss cheese, crumbled
- 1/2 teaspoon cayenne pepper
- 40 grams Swiss chard, torn into pieces
- 2 large eggs
- 60 grams yellow onions, chopped
- 1 teaspoon fine sea salt

1. Preheat oven to 175 degrees Celsius.
2. Grease a 9x13 inch baking dish with olive oil.
3. In a large bowl, whisk together the eggs, crème fraiche, salt, black pepper, and cayenne pepper.
4. Stir in the Swiss cheese, Swiss chard, and onions.
5. Pour the egg mixture into the prepared baking dish.
6. Bake for 18 minutes, or until the eggs are set and the top is golden brown.
7. Let cool for a few minutes before serving.

PARMESAN CAULIFLOWER

PREP TIME: 12 MINUTES | COOK TIME: 20 MINUTES | SERVES 4

- 4 cups cauliflower florets
- 100g whole-wheat bread crumbs
- 1 teaspoon coarse sea salt or kosher salt
- 25g Parmesan cheese, grated
- 4 tablespoons butter
- 4 tablespoons mild hot sauce
- Olive oil spray

The Complete UK Tower Air Fryer Cookbook

1. Place a parchment liner in the air fryer basket.
2. Cut the cauliflower florets in half and set them aside.
3. In a small bowl, mix the bread crumbs, salt, and Parmesan; set aside.
4. In a small microwave-safe bowl, combine the hot sauce and butter. Heat in the microwave until the butter is melted, about 30 seconds. Whisk.
5. Holding the stems of the cauliflower florets, dip them in the butter mixture to coat. Shake off any excess mixture.
6. Dredge the dipped florets with the bread crumb mixture, then put them in the air fryer basket. There's no need for a single layer; just toss them all in there.
7. Spray the cauliflower lightly with olive oil and air fry at 175°C for 15 minutes, shaking the basket a few times throughout the cooking process. The florets are done when they are lightly browned and crispy. Serve warm.

CREAM BUNS WITH STRAWBERRIES

PREP TIME: 10 MINUTES | COOK TIME: 12 MINUTES | SERVES 6

- 240g all-purpose flour
- 50g granulated sugar
- 8g baking powder
- 1g of salt
- 85g chopped cold butter
- 84g chopped fresh strawberries
- 120 ml whipping cream
- 2 large eggs
- 10 ml vanilla extract
- 5 ml of water

1. Sift the flour, sugar, baking powder, and salt into a large bowl. Rub in the butter with your fingertips or a food processor until the mixture resembles fine crumbs.
2. Stir in the strawberries. Set aside.
3. In a separate bowl, beat the whipping cream, 1 egg, and vanilla extract until soft peaks form.
4. Add the cream mixture to the flour mixture and mix until just combined. Spread the mixture out to a thickness of 1.5 inches (38 mm).
5. Use a round cookie cutter to cut out the buns. Brush the tops of the buns with a mixture of egg and water.
6. Preheat the air fryer to 190 degrees Celsius (375 degrees Fahrenheit).
7. Line the air fryer basket with parchment paper. Place the buns on the parchment paper and cook for 12 minutes, or until golden brown.

ONION RINGS

PREP TIME: 7 MINUTES | COOK TIME: 10 MINUTES | SERVES 3

- 1 onion, cut into slices, separate into rings
- 250ml milk
- 150g pork rinds, crushed
- 175g almond flour
- 1 egg
- 1 tablespoon baking powder
- 1/2 teaspoon salt

1. Preheat your air fryer for 10 minutes. Slice the onion, then separate into rings. In a bowl, whisk together the baking powder, flour, and salt.
2. Beat in the eggs and milk, then add to the flour mixture. Dip the onion rings into the batter to coat them.
3. Spread the pork rinds on a plate and dip the rings into the crumbs. Place the onion rings in your air fryer and cook for 10 minutes at 180°C.

SPICED NUTS

PREP TIME: 7 MINUTES | COOK TIME: 25 MINUTES | SERVES 3

- 250g almonds
- 200g pecan halves
- 150g cashews
- 1 egg white, beaten
- 1/2 teaspoon ground cinnamon
- Pinch cayenne pepper
- 1/4 teaspoon ground cloves
- Pinch salt

1. Combine the egg white with spices. Preheat your air fryer to 150°C/300°F.
2. Toss the nuts in the spiced mixture. Cook for 25 minutes, stirring throughout cooking time.

FRENCH TOAST IN STICKS

PREP TIME: 5 MINUTES | COOK TIME: 10 MINUTES | SERVES 4

- 4 slices of white bread, 38 mm thick, preferably hard
- 2 eggs
- 60 ml of milk
- 15 ml maple sauce
- 2 ml vanilla extract
- Nonstick Spray Oil
- 38g of sugar
- 3 ground cinnamon
- Maple syrup, to serve
- Sugar to sprinkle

1. Cut each slice of bread into thirds making 12 pieces. Place sideways.
2. Beat the eggs, milk, maple syrup and vanilla extract in a bowl.
3. Preheat your air fryer to 165°C.
4. Dip the sliced bread in the egg mixture and place it in the preheated air fryer. Sprinkle French toast generously with oil spray. Cook French toast for 10 minutes at 165°C. Turn the toast halfway through cooking.
5. Mix the sugar and cinnamon in a bowl. Cover the French toast with the sugar and cinnamon mixture when you have finished cooking.

6. Serve with Maple syrup and sprinkle with powdered sugar.

GARLIC CAULIFLOWER NUGGETS

PREP TIME: 7 MINUTES | COOK TIME: 20 MINUTES | SERVES 4

- 1 head cauliflower, chopped in a food processor
- 75g Parmesan cheese, grated
- Salt and pepper to taste
- 60g almond flour
- 2 eggs
- 1 teaspoon garlic, minced

1. Mix all the ingredients. Shape into nuggets and spray with olive oil. Preheat your air fryer to 200°C.
2. Cook for 10 minutes on each side.

CHICKPEA & ZUCCHINI BURGERS

PREP TIME: 10 MINUTES | COOK TIME: 10 MINUTES | SERVES 4

- 400g chickpeas, drained and rinsed
- 1 small red onion, diced
- 2 eggs, beaten
- 50g almond flour
- 3 tablespoons coriander
- 1 teaspoon garlic puree
- 50g cheddar cheese, grated
- 1 small courgette, spiralized
- 1 teaspoon chili powder
- Salt and pepper to taste
- 1 teaspoon mixed spice

1. Add all of the ingredients to a bowl and mix well.
2. Shape the mixture into burger patties.
3. Preheat your air fryer to 180°C (350°F).
4. Cook the burgers in the air fryer for 15 minutes, or until cooked through.
5. Serve hot.

BROCCOLI WITH CHEESE & OLIVES

PREP TIME: 10 MINUTES | COOK TIME: 15 MINUTES | SERVES 4

- 900g broccoli florets
- 50g Parmesan cheese, shaved
- 2 teaspoons lemon zest, grated
- 75g kalamata olives, halved and pitted
- 1 teaspoon black pepper
- 1 teaspoon sea salt
- 2 tablespoons olive oil

1. Bring a pot of water to the boil and cook the broccoli for 4 minutes. Drain the broccoli and set aside.
2. Toss the broccoli with the olive oil, salt, and pepper.
3. Place the broccoli in the air fryer basket and cook for 15 minutes at 200°C (400°F). Toss twice during cooking time.
4. Transfer the broccoli to a serving bowl and toss with the lemon zest, olives, and Parmesan cheese.

VEGETABLE FRIES

PREP TIME: 10 MINUTES | COOK TIME: 18 MINUTES | SERVES 4

- 150g sweet potatoes, peeled and chopped into chips
- 150g courgette, peeled and chopped into chips
- 150g carrots, peeled and chopped into chips
- 2 tablespoons olive oil
- Salt and pepper to taste
- Pinch of basil
- Pinch of mixed spice

1. Toss the vegetables in the olive oil and season with salt, pepper, basil, and mixed spice.
2. Place the vegetables in the air fryer basket and cook at 180°C (360°F) for 18 minutes, or until the vegetables are tender and slightly crispy.
3. Toss the vegetables halfway through cooking time.
4. Serve immediately.

CRAB & CHEESE SOUFFLÉ

PREP TIME: 10 MINUTES | COOK TIME: 18 MINUTES | SERVES 2

- 500g cooked crab meat
- 1 red pepper, diced
- 1 small onion, diced
- 250ml double cream
- 250ml milk
- 110g brie cheese
- 4 eggs
- 5 drops liquid sweetener
- 75g cheddar cheese, grated
- 4 cups bread, cubed

1. Soak the crab meat in brandy and enough water to cover the crab. Once the crab has soaked for 30 minutes, drain it and set aside.
2. In a large frying pan, melt some butter and add the onion. Cook until softened, then add the bread cubes and cook for a further 2 minutes.
3. Add the crab meat to the pan and stir to combine. Add half of the milk and 1 tablespoon of brandy and cook for 2 minutes.
4. Add the remaining bread cubes and stir to combine. Sprinkle with cheddar cheese and pepper.
5. Divide the stuffing between 5 ramekins, without brushing them with oil. Distribute the brie cheese evenly.
6. In a bowl, combine the remaining cream with the sweetener. Heat the cream in a pan and add the remaining milk. Pour the mixture over the ramekins.
7. Preheat your air fryer to 175°C (350°F). Place the ramekins in the air fryer basket and cook for 20 minutes, or until the cheese is melted and golden brown.
8. Serve immediately.

BAKED TOMATO & EGG

PREP TIME: 10 MINUTES | COOK TIME: 20 MINUTES | SERVES 2

- 2 tomatoes
- 4 eggs
- 100g mozzarella cheese, shredded
- Salt and pepper to taste
- 1 tablespoon olive oil
- A few basil leaves

1. Preheat your air fryer to 180°C (360°F).
2. Cut each tomato in half and place them in a bowl. Season with salt and pepper.
3. Place the cheese around the bottom of the tomatoes and add the basil leaves.
4. Break one egg into each tomato slice.

5. Garnish with cheese and drizzle with olive oil.
6. Cook in the air fryer for 20 minutes, or until the eggs are cooked to your liking.
7. Serve immediately.

SPICY MOZZARELLA STICK

PREP TIME: 10 MINUTES | COOK TIME: 5 MINUTES | SERVES 3

- 200g mozzarella cheese, cut into strips
- 2 tablespoons olive oil
- 1/2 teaspoon salt
- 100g pork rinds, crushed
- 1 egg
- 1 teaspoon garlic powder
- 1 teaspoon paprika

1. Cut the mozzarella into 6 strips.
2. Whisk the egg with the salt, paprika, and garlic powder.
3. Dip the mozzarella strips into the egg mixture, then into the crushed pork rinds.
4. Arrange the mozzarella sticks on a baking sheet and place in the fridge for 30 minutes.
5. Preheat your air fryer to 180°C (360°F).

The Complete UK Tower Air Fryer Cookbook

6. Drizzle olive oil into the air fryer basket.
7. Arrange the mozzarella sticks in the air fryer basket and cook for about 5 minutes. Make sure to turn them at least twice, to ensure they will become golden on all sides.
8. Serve immediately.

AIR-FRIED WALNUTS & GREEN BEANS

PREP TIME: 10 MINUTES | COOK TIME: 20 MINUTES | SERVES 5

- 1/2 teaspoon chili powder
- 200g green beans, trimmed and cut into 3-inch long pieces
- 50g walnuts, roasted and roughly chopped
- 4 garlic cloves, minced
- 1 tablespoon light soy sauce
- 1 teaspoon sugar-free maple syrup
- 1 teaspoon sesame oil
- Salt and pepper to taste

1. Wash and trim the green beans.
2. In a bowl, combine the green beans, walnuts, garlic, soy sauce, maple syrup, sesame oil, salt, and pepper.
3. Preheat your air fryer to 190°C (390°F).
4. Add the marinated green beans and walnuts to the air fryer basket and spray with sesame oil.
5. Cook for 20 minutes, shaking the basket halfway through cooking time.
6. Serve warm.

AIR-FRIED BANANA TURMERIC CHIPS

PREP TIME: 10 MINUTES | COOK TIME: 8 MINUTES | SERVES 4

- 10mg of sesame oil
- 5mg pepper
- 1 teaspoon turmeric
- 4 large bananas, sliced
- ½ teaspoon salt
- 2 teaspoons agave syrup

1. In a bowl, combine the agave syrup, turmeric powder, salt, and pepper. Add the sliced bananas and toss to coat.
2. Preheat your air fryer to 190°C (370°F).
3. Spray the sesame oil over the sliced bananas and place them in the air fryer basket.
4. Cook for 8 minutes, shaking the basket halfway through cooking time.
5. Serve warm.

TOMATO VEGETABLE CURRY

PREP TIME: 10 MINUTES | COOK TIME: 25 MINUTES | SERVES 4

- 1 teaspoon dried oregano
- 1 tablespoon basil leaves, chopped
- 1 tablespoon cilantro leaves, chopped
- 2 teaspoons curry powder
- 2 cloves garlic, minced
- 1 large onion, diced
- 75g chickpeas, soaked and rinsed
- 125ml water
- 125ml coconut milk

- 75g potatoes, diced
- 125g tomatoes, chopped

1. Cut the washed vegetables into small cubes. Chop the herbs into small pieces and set aside.
2. Add the coconut milk and water to the air fryer basket.
3. Add the garlic, onions, and cubed vegetables. Season with curry powder, pepper, and oregano.
4. Cook for 20 minutes, stirring halfway through cooking time.
5. Add the basil and cilantro leaves. Cook for another 5 minutes, or until the soup thickens.
6. Serve warm with jasmine rice.

AIR-FRIED CARROTS WITH LEMON

PREP TIME: 10 MINUTES | COOK TIME: 18 MINUTES | SERVES 4

- 200g carrots, julienned
- 1 tablespoon parsley, chopped
- 1 teaspoon paprika
- 2 teaspoons lemon juice
- 1/2 teaspoon black pepper
- 10mg salt
- 2 teaspoons olive oil
- 1 tablespoon lemon zest

1. In a bowl, combine the lemon zest, lemon juice, paprika, salt, pepper, olive oil, and carrots. Toss to coat.
2. Allow the carrots to marinate for 30 minutes.
3. Preheat your air fryer to 190°C (390°F).
4. Add the carrots to the air fryer basket and cook for 18 minutes.
5. Shake the basket halfway through cooking time.
6. Serve warm.

POTATO FRIES WITH BEAN SPROUTS & PEANUT HERB SALAD

PREP TIME: 10 MINUTES | COOK TIME: 20 MINUTES | SERVES 4

300g sweet potato, cut into fries
150g bean sprouts
2 tablespoons parsley leaves, chopped
2 tablespoons basil leaves, chopped
1 teaspoon salt
1 teaspoon pepper
1 tablespoon sriracha sauce
1 tablespoon rice vinegar
50g roasted peanuts
2 teaspoons olive oil

1. Preheat your air fryer to 190°C (390°F).
2. Place the sweet potato fries in the air fryer basket and spray with olive oil. Season with salt.
3. Cook for 15 minutes, shaking the basket halfway through cooking time.
4. While the sweet potato fries are cooking, roast the peanuts. Preheat your air fryer to 200°C (400°F). Place the peanuts in the air fryer basket and spray with olive oil. Cook for 5 minutes, or until golden brown.
5. In a large bowl, combine the bean sprouts, parsley, basil, salt, pepper, sriracha sauce, and rice vinegar.
6. Add the sweet potato fries and roasted peanuts and toss to coat.
7. Serve immediately.

CHAPTER 2:
BREAKFASTS

BEST-EVER EGG MUFFINS

PREP TIME: 10 MINUTES | COOK TIME: 20 MINUTES | MAKES 8 MUFFINS

- 2 cups peeled, cubed butternut squash (about 450 grams)
- 2 large eggs
- 259g egg whites
- 100 grams shredded low-sodium cheddar cheese
- 2 cups chopped broccoli florets (about 250 grams)
- 2 teaspoons dried oregano
- ¼ teaspoon freshly ground black pepper
- ¼ teaspoon sea salt

1. Preheat the air fryer to 200 degrees Celsius.
2. Arrange the butternut squash in a single layer in the air fryer basket and cook for 10 minutes.
3. Meanwhile, in a large bowl, whisk together the eggs and egg whites. Add the cheddar cheese, broccoli, oregano, black pepper, and salt to the eggs and stir to combine.
4. Carefully transfer the butternut squash to the egg mixture.
5. Arrange 8 silicone muffin cups in a single layer in the basket. Divide the egg mixture between the cups, making sure not to overfill them.
6. Reduce the air fryer temperature to 160 degrees Celsius (320 degrees Fahrenheit) and cook for 10 minutes. The muffins are done when a knife inserted into the center comes out clean.

ZUCCHINI QUICHE WITH SWEET POTATO "CRUST"

PREP TIME: 10 MINUTES | COOK TIME: 25 MINUTES | SERVES 4

- 2 large sweet potatoes, cut into 1 cm thick slices
- 30 ml avocado oil cooking spray
- 20 egg whites
- 60 ml unsweetened almond milk
- 2 medium zucchini, chopped
- 500 g cherry tomatoes, quartered
- 750 g fresh spinach
- 1 small shallot, finely diced
- 1 garlic clove, minced
- 1/2 teaspoon red pepper flakes
- 1/2 teaspoon dried oregano
- 1/4 teaspoon sea salt
- 1 medium roma tomato, sliced

1. Preheat the air fryer to 200 degrees Celsius.
2. Working in batches if necessary, arrange the sweet potato slices in an air fryer baking dish, overlapping them slightly to form a single crust-like layer. Spray with avocado oil. Place the baking dish in the air fryer basket and cook for 10 minutes.
3. Meanwhile, in a large bowl, whisk together the egg whites and almond milk. Add the zucchini, cherry tomatoes, spinach, shallot, garlic, red pepper flakes, oregano, and salt and stir to combine.
4. Once the crust is done, carefully pour the egg mixture into the crust. Top the quiche with the tomato slices.
5. Place the baking dish back in the basket, decrease the temperature to 175 degrees Celsius (350 degrees Fahrenheit), and cook for 10 to 15 minutes. The quiche is done when a knife inserted near the center comes out clean. Let it rest for 10 minutes before serving.

CHEESY FRITTATA

PREP TIME: 10 MINUTES | COOK TIME: 20 MINUTES | SERVES 4

- 4 large eggs
- 1 green onion, chopped
- 2 tablespoons roasted red bell pepper, chopped
- 100 grams cheddar cheese, shredded
- 125 grams cooked, crumbled low-sodium breakfast sausage
- A pinch of cayenne pepper
- Cooking spray

1. Combine all of the ingredients in a bowl.
2. Preheat the air fryer to 180 degrees Celsius (360 degrees Fahrenheit).
3. Grease a small cake pan with cooking spray.

4. Pour the mixture into the pan.
5. Cook in the air fryer for 20 minutes, or until the eggs are set and the cheese is melted.
6. Garnish with chopped parsley, if desired.

OATMEAL WITH STRAWBERRIES

PREP TIME: 5 MINUTES | COOK TIME: 15 MINUTES | SERVES 4

- 100g shredded coconut
- 60g berries
- 500ml coconut milk
- 1/4 teaspoon vanilla extract
- 4 tablespoons stevia
- Cooking spray

1. Grease the air fryer basket with cooking spray.
2. Add all of the ingredients to the air fryer basket and stir to combine.
3. Cook at 180°C for 15 minutes, or until the coconut is golden brown and the berries are soft.
4. Serve immediately.

KETO BREAKFAST BACON

PREP TIME: 10 MINUTES | COOK TIME: 10 MINUTES | SERVES 4

- 225g bacon, sliced
- 1 teaspoon dried oregano
- 0.5 teaspoon ground black pepper
- 0.5 teaspoon salt
- 0.5 teaspoon ground thyme
- 100g cheddar cheese, grated

1. Preheat your air fryer to 180°C (360°F).
2. Slice the bacon and rub it with the dried oregano, ground black pepper, salt, and ground thyme on each side. Leave the bacon for 3 minutes to soak in the spices.
3. Place the sliced bacon in the air fryer basket and cook for 5 minutes.
4. Sprinkle the bacon with the grated cheddar cheese and cook for an additional 30 seconds, or until the cheese is melted and bubbly.
5. Transfer to serving plates and serve warm.

BUCKWHEAT CREPES

PREP TIME: 10 MINUTES | COOK TIME: 12 MINUTES | SERVES 6

- 250g untoasted buckwheat flour
- 60g flaxseed meal
- 420ml light (canned) coconut milk
- 1 tablespoon avocado oil
- 1/8 teaspoon ground cinnamon
- 1 tablespoon coconut sugar

1. Preheat your air fryer to 150°C.
2. In a blender, combine the buckwheat flour, coconut sugar, coconut milk, cinnamon, avocado oil, and flaxseed meal. Blend until smooth and lump-free.
3. Pour 1/4 cup of batter onto a parchment paper round.
4. Swirl the paper to spread the batter into a thin round crepe.

5. Cook in the air fryer for 3 minutes, or until golden brown.
6. Carefully transfer the crepe to a plate using a spatula.
7. Repeat steps 3-6 with the rest of the batter.
8. Serve the crepes with your favorite compote, jam, or fruits.

SAUSAGE BISCUIT

PREP TIME: 5 MINUTES | COOK TIME: 20 MINUTES | SERVES 2

- 2 eggs
- 225g sausage meat
- ½ teaspoon salt
- ¼ teaspoon pepper
- ½ tablespoon butter
- 1 x 340g can of ready-rolled flaky pastry
- ¼ cup grated cheddar cheese

1. Preheat your air fryer to 180°C.
2. In a skillet, brown the sausage meat over medium heat, breaking it up into crumbles.
3. In a bowl, whisk the eggs with the salt and pepper.
4. Melt the butter in a pan over medium heat. Add the eggs and cook, stirring constantly, until scrambled.
5. Remove one sheet of pastry from the can and cut it in half lengthways. Place one half on a work surface. Spread the sausage meat mixture over the pastry, leaving a 1cm border. Sprinkle with the cheese.
6. Fold the other half of the pastry over the filling and pinch the edges together to seal.
7. Cut the sausage roll into 6 equal pieces.
8. Place the sausage rolls in the air fryer basket, spacing them apart.
9. Cook for 5 minutes, or until golden brown.

HOMEMADE GRANOLA

PREP TIME: 5 MINUTES | COOK TIME: 15 MINUTES | SERVES 12

- 100g dried berries
- 3 cups rolled oats
- 50g pumpkin seeds
- 50g honey
- 50g chia seeds
- 100g almonds
- 50g olive oil
- 1/4 teaspoon salt
- Pumpkin spice, to taste

1. Preheat your air fryer to 160°C.
2. In a large bowl, combine the oats, pumpkin seeds, chia seeds, almonds, salt, and pumpkin spice.
3. Pour the oil and honey into the bowl and mix well until everything is well coated.
4. Line a baking sheet with parchment paper and spread out the oat mixture in one layer. Use a spoon to press down evenly to ensure that it is even throughout.
5. Cook in the air fryer for 15 minutes, or until golden brown and fragrant.
6. Remove from the air fryer and let cool completely.
7. Break into clusters and enjoy!

BREAKFAST PIZZA

PREP TIME: 5 MINUTES | COOK TIME: 15 MINUTES | SERVES 4

- 150g sausage, crumbled
- 1 sheet of crescent dough
- 100g cheddar cheese, grated
- 100g mozzarella cheese, grated
- 3 eggs, scrambled
- 1/2 chopped bell pepper

1. Preheat your air fryer to 175°C.
2. Lightly grease a pie pan with oil.
3. Spread the crescent dough evenly in the pan.

4. Cook in the air fryer for 5 minutes, or until the top is slightly browned.
5. Remove from the air fryer.
6. Top with the eggs, sausage, bell pepper, and cheeses.
7. Return to the air fryer for an additional 5-10 minutes, or until golden brown.

ALL BERRIES PANCAKES

PREP TIME: 15 MINUTES | COOK TIME: 10 MINUTES | SERVES 4

- 120g frozen blueberries, thawed
- 120g frozen cranberries, thawed
- 250ml coconut milk
- 40g coconut oil, melted, for greasing
- 40g stevia
- 150g whole wheat flour, finely milled
- 2 teaspoons baking powder
- 1 teaspoon vanilla extract
- ¼ teaspoon salt

1. Preheat your air fryer to 170°C
2. Grease an air fryer basket with a little coconut oil.
3. In a bowl, whisk together the coconut oil, coconut milk, flour, stevia, baking powder, vanilla extract, and salt. Gently fold in the berries.

4. Divide the batter into equal portions and pour into the prepared air fryer basket.
5. Cook for 3-4 minutes per side, or until golden brown and cooked through.
6. Transfer to a plate and sprinkle with palm sugar. Serve.

LOW-CARB WHITE EGG AND SPINACH FRITTATA

PREP TIME: 12-15 MINUTES | COOK TIME: 12 MINUTES | SERVES 4

- 8 egg whites
- 200g fresh spinach
- 40ml olive oil
- 1 green pepper, chopped
- 1 red pepper, chopped
- 125g feta cheese, reduced-fat, crumbled
- 50g yellow onion, chopped
- 1 teaspoon salt
- 1 teaspoon pepper

1. Preheat your air fryer to 170°C.
2. Meanwhile, place the red and green peppers and onion in the air fryer basket and cook for 3 minutes. Season with salt and pepper.
3. Pour the egg whites into the air fryer basket and cook for 4 minutes. Add the spinach and feta cheese on top.
4. Cook for a further 5 minutes, or until the egg whites are set.
5. Transfer to a plate, slice, and serve.

PUMPKIN PIE FRENCH TOAST

PREP TIME: 10 MINUTES | COOK TIME: 20 MINUTES | SERVES 4

- 2 large eggs, beaten
- 4 slices of cinnamon swirl bread
- 150ml semi-skimmed milk
- 150g pumpkin puree

- 1/4 teaspoon ground cinnamon
- 1/4 teaspoon ground ginger
- 1/4 teaspoon ground nutmeg
- 50g salted butter, melted

1. In a large mixing bowl, whisk together the pumpkin puree, milk, eggs, cinnamon, ginger, and nutmeg until smooth. Dip the bread in the egg mixture on both sides.
2. Place the rack inside of the air fryer's cooking basket. Place 2 slices of bread onto the rack. Set the temperature to 170°C/340°F for 10 minutes. Serve pumpkin pie toast with butter.

BAKED MINI QUICHE

PREP TIME: 10 MINUTES | COOK TIME: 15 MINUTES | SERVES 2

- 2 large eggs
- 1 large yellow onion, diced
- 225g whole-wheat flour
- 150g butter, softened
- 1 teaspoon salt
- 60ml milk
- 2 tablespoons olive oil
- 112g cottage cheese
- Salt and black pepper, to taste

1. Preheat your air fryer to 180°C.
2. In a large bowl, combine the flour, butter, salt, and milk. Knead the dough until smooth. Wrap the dough in cling film and refrigerate for 15 minutes.
3. Heat the olive oil in a frying pan over medium heat. Add the onion and cook until softened. Add the spinach and cook until wilted. Drain the excess moisture from the spinach.
4. In a separate bowl, whisk together the eggs and cottage cheese. Season with salt and pepper.
5. Remove the dough from the fridge and divide it into eight equal parts. Roll out each piece of dough into a circle that will fit into the bottom of a muffin tin. Place the dough circles in the muffin tins.
6. Top the dough with the spinach mixture and then the egg mixture.
7. Place the muffin tins in the air fryer basket and cook for 15 minutes, or until the quiche is set.
8. Remove the quiche from the muffin tins and serve warm or cold.

BREAKFAST CHICKEN HASH

PREP TIME: 10 MINUTES | COOK TIME: 14 MINUTES | SERVES 3

- 170g cauliflower, chopped
- 200g chicken fillet, chopped
- 1 tablespoon water
- 1 green pepper, chopped
- 1/2 yellow onion, diced
- 1 teaspoon ground black pepper
- 3 tablespoons butter
- 1 tablespoon cream

1. Chop the cauliflower and place in a food processor. Pulse until it resembles rice.
2. Chop the chicken fillet into small pieces. Sprinkle the chicken fillet with ground black pepper and stir.
3. Preheat your air fryer to 190°C. Dice the yellow onion and chop the green pepper. In a large mixing bowl, combine the cauliflower rice, chicken, onion, pepper, butter, and cream.
4. Add the mixture to the air fryer basket and cook for 15-20 minutes, or until the chicken is cooked through and the vegetables are tender.

EGGS AND COCOTTE ON TOAST

PREP TIME: 10 MINUTES | COOK TIME: 10 MINUTES | SERVES 2

- ¼ teaspoon black pepper
- 5mg salt
- ½ teaspoon Italian seasoning
- ¼ teaspoon balsamic vinegar
- ¼ teaspoon sugar-free maple syrup

- 100g sausages, chopped into small pieces
- 2 large eggs
- 2 slices wholemeal toast
- 3 tablespoons cheddar cheese, grated
- 6 slices tomatoes
- Cooking spray
- A little mayonnaise to serve

1. Spray a baking dish with cooking spray. Place the toast slices at the bottom of the dish.
2. Sprinkle the sausages over the toast. Lay the tomatoes over it. Sprinkle the top with cheese.
3. Beat the eggs and then pour over the top of the bread slices. Drizzle vinegar and maple syrup over the eggs.
4. Season with Italian seasoning, salt, and pepper, then sprinkle some more cheese on top.
5. Place the baking dish in the air fryer basket that should be preheated to 160°C/320°F and cook for 10 minutes.
6. Remove from the air fryer and add a touch of mayonnaise and serve.

STRAWBERRIES OATMEAL

PREP TIME: 5 MINUTES | COOK TIME: 15 MINUTES | SERVES 4

- 100g shredded coconut
- 50g strawberries, hulled and halved
- 500ml coconut milk
- ¼ teaspoon vanilla extract
- 4 teaspoons stevia
- Cooking spray

1. Grease the air fryer's pan with cooking spray. Add all the ingredients to the pan and toss to coat.
2. Cook at 180°C for 15 minutes, or until the coconut is golden brown and the strawberries are soft.
3. Divide the pudding into bowls and serve.

BAGELS

PREP TIME: 20 MINUTES | COOK TIME: 20 MINUTES | SERVES 12

- 250g (9oz) strong white bread flour
- 7g (1/4oz) active dry yeast
- 1 teaspoon brown sugar
- 125ml (4.25fl oz) lukewarm water
- 1 tablespoon olive oil, plus extra for greasing
- 1 teaspoon salt
- 1 large egg, beaten

1. In a large bowl, dissolve the yeast and sugar in the lukewarm water. Let stand for 5 minutes, or until foamy.
2. Stir in the flour, olive oil, and salt until a dough forms.
3. Turn the dough out onto a lightly floured surface and knead for 5-10 minutes, or until smooth and elastic.
4. Place the dough in a greased bowl, cover with plastic wrap, and let rise in a warm place for 1 hour, or until doubled in size.
5. Punch down the dough and divide it into 5 equal pieces.
6. Roll each piece of dough into a smooth ball.

7. Place the bagels on a baking sheet lined with parchment paper.
8. Preheat the air fryer to 180 degrees Celsius (350 degrees Fahrenheit).
9. Cook the bagels for 10-12 minutes, or until golden brown.
10. Let the bagels cool slightly before serving.

BREAKFAST HASH

PREP TIME: 10 MINUTES | COOK TIME: 8 MINUTES | SERVES 4

- 200g bacon, cooked
- 1 medium zucchini, cubed into small pieces
- 100g cheddar cheese, shredded
- 2 tablespoons butter
- 1 teaspoon ground thyme
- 1 teaspoon cilantro
- 1 teaspoon paprika
- 1 teaspoon ground black pepper
- 1 teaspoon salt

1. Preheat your air fryer to 200°C.
2. Chop the zucchini into small cubes and sprinkle with ground black pepper, salt, paprika, cilantro and ground thyme.
3. Add the butter to the air fryer basket tray and melt.
4. Add the zucchini cubes to the air fryer basket and cook for 5 minutes, or until softened.
5. Add the bacon to the zucchini cubes and stir to combine.
6. Sprinkle the zucchini mixture with shredded cheese and cook for a further 3 minutes, or until the cheese is melted and golden brown.
7. Transfer the breakfast hash to serving bowls and enjoy.

NO-BUN BREAKFAST BACON BURGER

PREP TIME: 10 MINUTES | COOK TIME: 8 MINUTES | SERVES 2

- 225g ground beef
- 1 egg, whisked
- 50g cooked, chopped bacon
- 1 teaspoon butter
- 1 teaspoon ground black pepper
- 1/2 teaspoon minced garlic
- 1/2 teaspoon salt
- 2 lettuce leaves
- 1/2 yellow onion, diced
- 1/2 cucumber, sliced finely
- 1/2 tomato, sliced finely

1. In a bowl, combine the ground beef, egg, bacon, butter, ground black pepper, minced garlic, and salt. Mix well and form into 2 patties.
2. Preheat your air fryer to 190°C. Spray the air fryer basket with olive oil and place the burgers inside of it. Cook the burgers for 8 minutes on each side, or until cooked through.
3. Meanwhile, slice the cucumber, onion, and tomato finely.
4. Place the tomato, onion, and cucumber onto the lettuce leaves.
5. When the burgers are cooked, allow them to cool slightly before placing them over the vegetables.
6. Serve immediately.

BREAKFAST SUGAR-FREE MAPLE CINNAMON BUNS

PREP TIME: 10 MINUTES | COOK TIME: 30 MINUTES | SERVES 9

- 375ml unsweetened almond milk, warmed slightly
- 4 tablespoons sugar-free maple syrup
- 1 ½ teaspoons active yeast
- 1 tablespoon ground flaxseed
- 3 tablespoons water
- 1 tablespoon coconut oil, melted
- 350g almond flour, sifted
- 225g wholemeal flour, sifted

- 3 teaspoons cinnamon powder
- 2 ripe bananas, sliced
- 4 dates, pitted
- 3 tablespoons icing sugar

1. In a large bowl, whisk together the almond milk, syrup, and yeast. Leave to stand for 10 minutes, or until the yeast is frothy.
2. In a separate bowl, whisk together the ground flaxseed and water. Leave to stand for 2 minutes, or until the flaxseed mixture has thickened.
3. Add the coconut oil to the yeast mixture and whisk to combine. Then, add the flaxseed mixture and whisk again.
4. Sift the almond flour, wholemeal flour, and 2 teaspoons of cinnamon powder into the wet ingredients. Mix until a dough forms.
5. Turn the dough out onto a lightly floured surface and knead for 10 minutes, or until smooth and elastic.
6. Place the dough in a greased bowl, cover with a tea towel, and leave in a warm place to rise for 1 hour, or until doubled in size.
7. Preheat your air fryer to 190°C. Once the dough has risen, roll it out on a lightly floured surface until it is about 30cm (12 inches) wide.
8. Spread the pecan, banana, and date mixture over the dough, leaving a 2cm (1 inch) border.
9. Roll up the dough from the long side and cut it into 9 equal slices.
10. Place the cinnamon rolls in a greased air fryer dish and cook for 30 minutes, or until golden brown.
11. Sprinkle the cinnamon rolls with icing sugar and serve warm.

QUINOA-CHICKEN MEATBALLS WITH GARLICKY ZUCCHINI SPIRALS

PREP TIME: 10 MINUTES | COOK TIME: 20 MINUTES | SERVES 4

- 75 g dry quinoa
- 4 medium zucchini, spiralized or peeled into ribbons
- 2 garlic cloves, minced
- 40 ml extra-virgin olive oil, plus more for misting
- 125 g canned low-sodium chickpeas, drained and rinsed
- 30 ml tahini
- 15 ml freshly squeezed lemon juice
- ¼ teaspoon sea salt
- 450 g ground chicken breast
- Chopped fresh parsley, for garnish

1. Preheat the air fryer to 175 degrees Celsius (350 degrees Fahrenheit). Cook the quinoa according to the package directions.
2. In a large bowl, stir together the zucchini, garlic, and olive oil.
3. Place the zucchini in the air fryer basket and cook for 8 minutes, stirring occasionally.
4. While the zucchini is cooking, in a large bowl, mash the chickpeas with a fork, then stir in the tahini, lemon juice, and salt until well combined and smooth.
5. Add the chicken and cooked quinoa and mix well. Using wet hands, form the mixture into about 16 (2.5 centimeter) meatballs.
6. Once the zucchini is done, transfer it to a bowl and mist with olive oil.
7. Working in batches if necessary, arrange the meatballs in a single layer in the air fryer basket. Set the temperature to 190 degrees Celsius (375 degrees Fahrenheit) and cook for 10 minutes, or until the internal temperature reaches 74 degrees Celsius (165 degrees Fahrenheit). Serve the meatballs over the zucchini and garnish with fresh parsley.

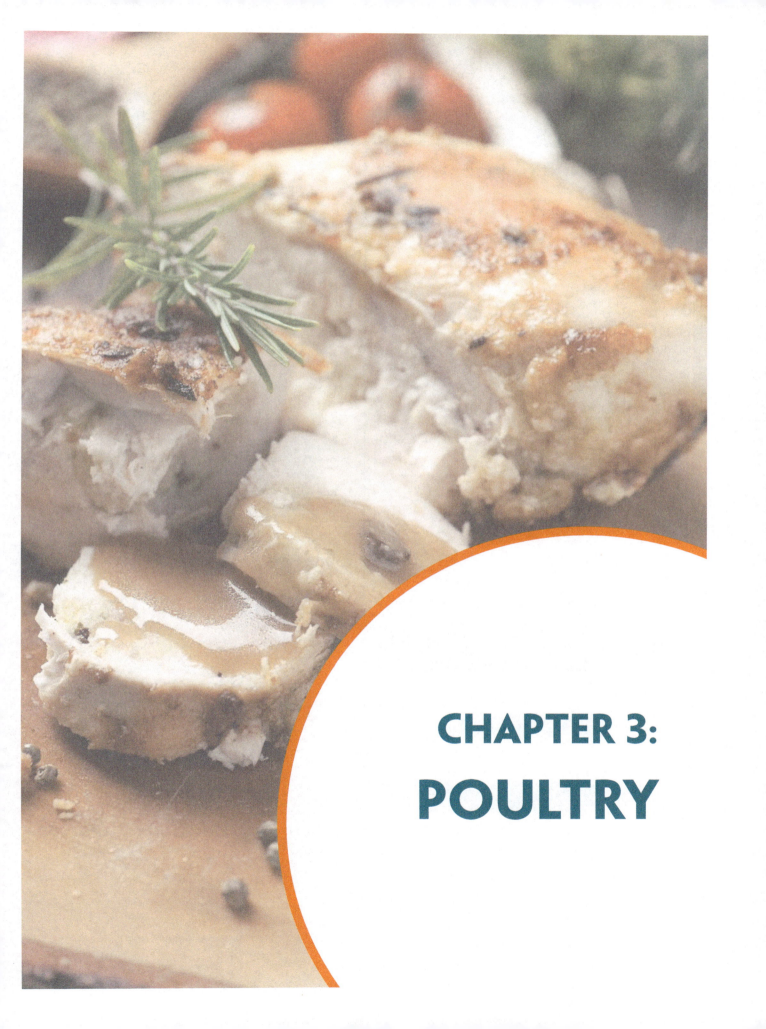

CHAPTER 3:
POULTRY

CHICKEN AND BROCCOLI

PREP TIME: 10 MINUTES | COOK TIME: 20 MINUTES | SERVES 4

- 1 onion, thinly sliced
- 2 cups broccoli florets
- 450 grams boneless, skinless chicken breast fillet, cut into cubes
- 10ml vegetable oil
- 5mg garlic powder
- 1 tablespoon ginger, minced
- 1 teaspoon low-sodium soy sauce
- 1 teaspoon sesame oil
- 2 teaspoons rice vinegar
- Lemon juice, for serving (optional)

1. Place the onion, broccoli, and chicken in a bowl and toss to coat.
2. In a separate bowl, whisk together the vegetable oil, garlic powder, ginger, soy sauce, sesame oil, and rice vinegar.
3. Pour the sauce mixture over the chicken and broccoli mixture and toss to coat.
4. Spread the chicken and broccoli mixture in a single layer in the air fryer basket.
5. Cook at 190 degrees Celsius for 20 minutes, or until the chicken is cooked through and the broccoli is tender.
6. Serve immediately, drizzled with lemon juice if desired.

CHICKEN CASSEROLE

PREP TIME: 10 MINUTES | COOK TIME: 9 MINUTES | SERVES 4

- 340g egg noodles
- 1/2 large onion, chopped
- 1/2 cup chopped carrots
- 100g frozen peas
- 100g frozen chopped broccoli
- 2 celery stalks, chopped
- 1.2 liters chicken broth
- 1 tablespoon garlic powder
- Salt and pepper to taste
- 1 cup cheddar cheese, grated
- 450g sliced French onions
- 1/2 pint soured cream
- 1 can mushroom-chicken cream soup

1. Preheat the air fryer to 180°C.
2. In the air fryer basket, combine the chicken broth, black pepper, salt, garlic powder, vegetables, and egg noodles.
3. Close and seal the air fryer basket.
4. Press the "Pressure Cook" button, choose 4 minutes of cooking time, and then press "Start."
5. When the air fryer beeps, perform a quick release and remove the basket.
6. Stir in the cheese, a third of the French onions, a can of soup, and the sour cream.
7. Gently fold in the remaining onion.
8. Close and seal the air fryer basket.
9. Press the "Air Fry" button and set the timer for 5 minutes, then press "Start."
10. When the air fryer beeps, remove the basket and serve.

BALSAMIC CHICKEN ROAST

PREP TIME: 20 MINUTES | COOK TIME: 1 HR. | SERVES 4

- 1 (1.8kg) whole chicken
- 1 tablespoon fresh rosemary, finely chopped
- 1 garlic clove, minced
- 1 tablespoon olive oil
- 5mg black pepper
- 8 sprigs fresh rosemary
- 10g balsamic vinegar
- 1 teaspoon brown sugar

1. Preheat your air fryer to 175°C.
2. In a small bowl, combine the garlic and rosemary.
3. Loosen the chicken skin by gently running your fingers underneath it.
4. Rub the olive oil and herb mixture all over the chicken flesh.

5. Place the chicken in a roasting pan and sprinkle with black pepper.
6. Stuff the chicken cavity with the rosemary sprigs and tie the legs together with kitchen twine.
7. Air fry the chicken for 1 hour, or until cooked through.
8. Baste the chicken with the pan juices every 15-20 minutes.
9. Meanwhile, in a small saucepan, combine the brown sugar and balsamic vinegar. Heat over medium heat, stirring constantly, until the sugar dissolves.
10. Remove the chicken from the air fryer and let it rest for 10 minutes.
11. Cut the chicken into smaller pieces and remove the skin.
12. Dip each piece of chicken in the balsamic vinegar glaze and garnish with rosemary.
13. Serve.

BUTTERMILK FRIED CHICKEN

PREP TIME: 10 MINUTES | COOK TIME: 15 MINUTES | SERVES 2

- 120ml low-fat buttermilk
- ¼ teaspoon hot sauce

- 100g boneless, skinless chicken breast, cut into 1-inch strips
- Cooking spray
- ¼ teaspoon salt
- ¼ teaspoon black pepper
- 60g cornflakes
- 30g stone-ground cornmeal
- ½ teaspoon garlic powder
- 1 teaspoon paprika

1. In a small bowl, combine the buttermilk and hot sauce. Add the chicken strips and toss to coat. Marinate for 15 minutes.
2. In a food processor, pulse the cornflakes until coarse crumbs form. Add the cornmeal, garlic powder, paprika, salt, and pepper and pulse until evenly mixed. Pour the crumbs into a shallow bowl.
3. Remove the chicken strips from the marinade and coat in the cornflake mixture.
4. Place the chicken strips in the air fryer basket and spray with nonstick cooking spray.
5. Cook at 190°C for 7 minutes, turning occasionally. Cook for an additional 7-10 minutes, or until cooked through and a meat thermometer inserted into the center registers 73°C.

TURKEY CROQUETTES

PREP TIME: 20 MINUTES | COOK TIME: 10 MINUTES | SERVES 4

- 50g grated Parmesan cheese
- 50g shredded Swiss cheese
- 1 tablespoon butter-flavored cooking spray
- 1/2 shallot, finely chopped
- 1 teaspoon minced fresh rosemary
- 250g mashed potatoes
- 1 tablespoon sour cream
- 1/2 teaspoon minced fresh sage
- 1/4 teaspoon salt
- 1/8 teaspoon black pepper
- 50g panko breadcrumbs
- 200g finely chopped cooked turkey
- 1 large egg
- 1 tablespoon water

1. Preheat your air fryer to 180°C/350°F.
2. In a large bowl, combine the mashed potatoes, Parmesan cheese, Swiss cheese, shallot, rosemary, sage, salt, and pepper. Mix until well combined.
3. Shape the mixture into 12 1-inch-thick patties.
4. In a shallow bowl, whisk together the egg and water. In another shallow bowl, place the panko breadcrumbs.
5. Dip each patty in the egg mixture, then coat in the panko breadcrumbs.
6. Place the coated patties in the air fryer basket.
7. Cook for 4-5 minutes, or until golden brown.
8. Turn the patties over and cook for an additional 4-5 minutes, or until golden brown and cooked through.
9. Serve immediately, garnished with sour cream if desired.

MINI TURKEY MEATBALLS

PREP TIME: 15 MINUTES | COOK TIME: 10 MINUTES | SERVES 5

- 3 tablespoons olive oil
- 3 tablespoons ketchup
- 3 garlic cloves, minced
- 1/4 teaspoon black pepper
- 50g grated Pecorino Romano
- 50g grated Parmesan
- 50g dried breadcrumbs
- 50g chopped Italian parsley
- 1 teaspoon salt
- 1 small onion, grated
- 450g ground dark turkey meat
- 1 large egg

1. In a large bowl, combine the pepper, salt, Pecorino, Parmesan, parsley, ketchup, breadcrumbs, egg, garlic, and onion. Mix well until combined.
2. Add the turkey and mix until well combined.
3. Shape the mixture into meatballs.

4. Air fry the meatballs at 180°C/360°F for 5 minutes, or until browned.
5. Prepare your favorite sauce and toss the meatballs in it.
6. Serve immediately.

HERBED CHICKEN MARSALA

PREP TIME: 10 MINUTES | COOK TIME: 30 MINUTES | SERVES 4

- 1 teaspoon kosher salt
- 1 teaspoon freshly ground black pepper
- 4 boneless, skinless chicken breast cutlets (about 160 grams each)
- 180 milliliters low-sodium chicken broth
- 2 teaspoons unsalted butter
- 2 tablespoons fresh flat-leaf parsley, roughly chopped
- 200 grams white button or cremini (baby Bella) mushrooms, sliced
- 75 grams whole wheat flour
- 75 milliliters sweet Marsala wine
- 75 milliliters sun-dried tomatoes (not packed in oil; not rehydrated), finely chopped or very thinly sliced
- 1/2 teaspoon chopped fresh rosemary
- 1 1/2 tablespoons extra-virgin olive oil

1. Pound the chicken cutlets to flatten them to about 1/2 cm thickness. Season with salt and pepper.
2. Coat the chicken cutlets in the flour.
3. Air fry the chicken cutlets at 180 degrees Celsius (350 degrees Fahrenheit) for 4 minutes, or until golden brown.
4. Transfer the chicken cutlets to an airtight container to keep warm.
5. In the air fryer basket, add the rosemary, sun-dried tomatoes, and 120 milliliters of the chicken broth. Cook for 1 minute, or until fragrant.
6. Add the mushrooms and cook for 5 minutes, or until softened.
7. Add the Marsala wine and cook for 1 minute, or until the sauce has thickened slightly.

8. Add the remaining 60 milliliters of chicken broth and the butter to the air fryer basket. Cook for 30 seconds, or until the butter has melted.
9. To serve, top the chicken cutlets with the sauce and mushrooms. Sprinkle with parsley.

TURKEY AND CREAM CHEESE BREAST PILLOWS

PREP TIME: 5 MINUTES | COOK TIME:10 MINUTES |SERVES 4

- 250 milliliters milk
- 1 large egg
- 80 milliliters water
- 60 milliliters olive oil or vegetable oil
- 2 teaspoons salt
- 4 tablespoons sugar
- 6 tablespoons dried yeast
- 500 grams all-purpose flour
- 1 egg yolk, beaten
- 2 jars cream cheese, softened
- 15 slices turkey breast, cut into quarters

1. In a large bowl, whisk together the milk, egg, water, olive oil, salt, sugar, and yeast.
2. Gradually add the flour, mixing until a soft dough forms.
3. Turn the dough out onto a lightly floured surface and knead for 5-7 minutes, or until smooth and elastic.
4. Place the dough in a greased bowl, cover with plastic wrap, and let rise in a warm place for 1 hour, or until doubled in size.
5. Punch down the dough and divide it into 15 equal pieces.
6. Roll out each piece of dough into a 10x10 cm square.
7. Place a piece of turkey breast and 1 teaspoon of cream cheese in the center of each square.
8. Fold the corners of the dough over the filling to form a square pillow.
9. Brush the tops of the pillows with the beaten egg yolk.
10. Preheat the air fryer to 180 degrees Celsius (350 degrees Fahrenheit).
11. Place 6 pillows in the air fryer basket and cook for 4-5 minutes, or until golden brown.
12. Repeat with the remaining pillows.
13. Serve warm.

CHICKEN TIKKA KEBAB

PREP TIME: 10 MINUTES | COOK TIME: 17 MINUTES | SERVES 4

- 450 grams boneless, skinless chicken thighs, cubed
- 1 tablespoon olive oil
- 1/2 cup red onion, diced
- 1/2 cup green bell pepper, diced
- 1/2 cup red bell pepper, diced
- Lime wedges and onion rounds to garnish

For Marinade:
- 125 milliliters Greek yogurt
- 21 grams grated ginger
- 21 grams minced garlic
- 15 milliliters lime juice
- 4 grams mild red chili powder
- 2 grams ground turmeric
- 5 grams garam masala
- 5 grams coriander powder
- 10 grams dried fenugreek leaves
- 5 grams salt

The Complete UK Tower Air Fryer Cookbook

BACON CHICKEN BREAST

1. Make the marinade by mixing all the ingredients in a bowl.
2. Add the chicken to the marinade and mix well to coat. Refrigerate for at least 8 hours, or overnight.
3. Add the onion, bell peppers, and oil to the marinade and mix well.
4. Thread the chicken, peppers, and onions onto skewers.
5. Preheat the air fryer to 180 degrees Celsius (350 degrees Fahrenheit).
6. Place the skewers in the air fryer basket and cook for 10 minutes.
7. Flip the skewers and cook for an additional 7 minutes, or until the chicken is cooked through.
8. Serve immediately with lime wedges and onion rounds.

SOY CHICKEN AND SESAME

PREP TIME: 10 MINUTES | COOK TIME: 50 MINUTES | SERVES 4

- 1 large chicken breast, cut into fillets
- 2 large eggs, beaten
- 100g breadcrumbs
- 1 teaspoon olive oil
- ¼ teaspoon salt
- Ground black pepper, to taste
- 100ml soy sauce
- 50g sesame seeds

1. Season the chicken fillets with salt and pepper.
2. In a shallow dish, combine the soy sauce and sesame seeds.
3. Dip the chicken fillets in the soy sauce mixture, then coat in the breadcrumbs.
4. Brush the chicken fillets with the beaten egg.
5. Air fry the chicken fillets at 180°C/360°F for 15-20 minutes, or until cooked through.
6. Serve immediately.

PREP TIME: 15 MINUTES | COOK TIME: 16 MINUTES | SERVES 4

- 500g skinless, boneless chicken breast
- 8 rashers bacon, halved lengthways
- 1 teaspoon paprika
- 5mg salt
- 1/2 teaspoon black pepper
- 1/2 teaspoon turmeric
- 1 tablespoon lemon juice
- 2 tablespoons butter, softened
- 1 teaspoon olive oil

1. Pound the chicken breast to flatten it.
2. Rub the chicken breast with the paprika, salt, pepper, and turmeric.
3. Sprinkle the chicken breast with lemon juice and place the butter in the center. Roll up the chicken breast and wrap it in the bacon.
4. Secure the bacon with toothpicks.
5. Preheat the air fryer to 190 degrees Celsius (380 degrees Fahrenheit).
6. Place the bacon-wrapped chicken breast in the air fryer basket and cook for 8 minutes.
7. Turn the chicken breast over and cook for 8 minutes more, or until cooked through.

CREAMY CHICKEN THIGHS

PREP TIME: 10 MINUTES | COOK TIME: 30 MINUTES | SERVES 2

- 1 tablespoon olive oil
- 6 bone-in, skin-on chicken thighs
- Salt
- Freshly ground black pepper
- 180 milliliters (¾ cup) low-sodium chicken broth
- 120 milliliters (½ cup) heavy cream
- 100 grams (½ cup) sun-dried tomatoes, chopped
- 30 grams (¼ cup) Parmesan cheese, grated
- Fresh basil leaves, to garnish

1. Preheat the air fryer to 180 degrees Celsius (350 degrees Fahrenheit).
2. Heat the olive oil in the air fryer basket.

3. Season the chicken thighs with salt and pepper.
4. Add the chicken thighs to the air fryer basket and cook for 5 minutes per side, or until browned.
5. Add the chicken broth, cream, sun-dried tomatoes, and Parmesan cheese to the air fryer basket.
6. Close the air fryer lid and cook for an additional 20 minutes, or until the chicken is cooked through.
7. Garnish with fresh basil leaves and serve.

TURKEY & CHEESE CALZONE

PREP TIME: 10 MINUTES | COOK TIME: 10 MINUTES | SERVES 4

- 1 free-range egg, beaten
- 20g grated mozzarella cheese
- 40g grated cheddar cheese
- 25g diced, cooked bacon
- 100g shredded cooked turkey
- 4 tablespoons tomato sauce
- Salt and pepper to taste
- 1 teaspoon thyme
- 1 teaspoon basil
- 1 teaspoon oregano
- 1 pack frozen pizza dough

1. Preheat your air fryer to 175°C.
2. Roll out the pizza dough into small circles, the same size as a small pizza.
3. In a bowl, combine the tomato sauce, thyme, oregano, and basil. Mix well.
4. Pour a small amount of the sauce mixture onto each pizza base and spread it evenly.
5. Top with the turkey, bacon, and cheeses.
6. Brush the edges of the dough with the beaten egg. Fold the dough in half and pinch the edges to seal.
7. Brush the outside of the calzones with the beaten egg.
8. Place the calzones in the air fryer basket and cook for 10 minutes, or until golden brown and cooked through.
9. Serve warm.

RANCH CHICKEN WINGS

PREP TIME: 10 MINUTES | COOK TIME: 35 MINUTES | SERVES 3

- 12 chicken wings
- 1 tablespoon olive oil
- 250 milliliters chicken broth
- 60 grams butter
- 125 milliliters red hot sauce
- 2 milliliters Worcestershire sauce
- 15 milliliters white vinegar
- 2 grams cayenne pepper
- 0.5 grams garlic powder
- Seasoned salt to taste
- Black pepper to taste
- Ranch dressing for dipping
- Celery sticks for garnish

1. Preheat the air fryer to 180 degrees Celsius (350 degrees Fahrenheit).
2. Place the chicken wings in the air fryer basket and pour the chicken broth into the bottom of the basket.

CHICKEN KEBABS

3. Close the air fryer and cook for 10 minutes.
4. Meanwhile, make the sauce by combining the cayenne pepper, butter, Worcestershire sauce, vinegar, garlic powder, and red hot sauce in a small saucepan. Heat over medium heat until the butter is melted and the sauce is hot.
5. Remove the chicken wings from the air fryer and set aside.
6. In a large bowl, toss the chicken wings with the olive oil, seasoned salt, and black pepper.
7. Return the chicken wings to the air fryer basket and cook for an additional 20 minutes, or until the wings are cooked through and crispy.
8. Transfer the chicken wings to the sauce and toss to coat.
9. Serve immediately with ranch dressing and celery sticks.

MOZZARELLA TURKEY ROLLS

PREP TIME: 10 MINUTES | COOK TIME: 10 MINUTES | SERVES 4

- 4 slices turkey breast
- 4 sprigs of chives (to tie rolls)
- 1 tomato, sliced
- 1/2 cup basil leaves, chopped
- 100g mozzarella cheese, sliced

1. Preheat your air fryer to 190°C (390°F).
2. Place the slices of mozzarella cheese, tomato, and basil leaves onto each slice of turkey breast. Roll up and secure with the chive sprigs.
3. Place the turkey rolls in the air fryer basket and cook for 10 minutes, or until the turkey is cooked through and the cheese is melted.
4. Serve warm.

PREP TIME: 10 MINUTES | COOK TIME: 15 MINUTES | SERVES 3

- 500g chicken breasts, diced
- 1 small courgette, sliced into rings
- 3 medium-sized bell peppers, sliced
- 2 medium tomatoes, sliced
- 6 large mushrooms, halved
- 1/4 cup sesame seeds
- 125ml soy sauce
- 20g honey
- 1 tablespoon olive oil
- Salt and pepper to taste
- Wooden skewers

1. Cut the chicken breasts into cubes and transfer to a mixing bowl. Season with salt and pepper. Add 1 tablespoon of olive oil and stir to blend. Add the soy sauce and honey and sprinkle with sesame seeds. Set aside for 30 minutes.
2. Alternately add the chicken pieces and vegetables to the wooden skewers.
3. Preheat your air fryer to 170°C (340°F).
4. Place the chicken kebabs in the air fryer basket and cook for 15 minutes, or until the chicken is cooked through and the vegetables are tender.
5. Serve hot.

CHAPTER 4:
BEEF, PORK AND LAMB

MUSTARD PORK TENDERLOIN

PREP TIME: 4 HOURS AND 10 MINUTES | COOK TIME: 20 MINUTES | SERVES 4

- 2 teaspoons light brown sugar
- 20g Dijon mustard
- ½ teaspoon dried thyme
- ¼ teaspoon dried parsley
- Salt and black pepper to taste
- 450 grams pork tenderloin

1. In a bowl, combine the light brown sugar, Dijon mustard, thyme, parsley, salt, and pepper.
2. Add the pork tenderloin to the bowl and coat it with the marinade.
3. Cover the bowl and refrigerate for at least 4 hours, or overnight.
4. Preheat the air fryer to 200 degrees Celsius (400 degrees Fahrenheit).
5. Remove the pork tenderloin from the marinade and place it in the air fryer basket.
6. Cook for 20 minutes, or until the pork tenderloin is cooked through.
7. Serve immediately.

DUMPLINGS WITH PORK

PREP TIME: 30 MINUTES | COOK TIME: 20 MINUTES | SERVES 4

- 18 dumpling wrappers
- 1 tablespoon olive oil
- 400g chopped bok choy
- 2 tablespoons rice vinegar
- 1 tablespoon chopped ginger
- 1/4 teaspoon red pepper flakes
- 1 tablespoon minced garlic
- 1/2 cup ground lean pork
- Cooking spray
- 2 teaspoons light soy sauce
- 1/2 teaspoon honey
- 1 tablespoon toasted sesame oil
- 1/8 cup chopped scallions

1. Preheat the air fryer to 205°C.
2. Heat the olive oil in a pan over medium heat. Add the bok choy, garlic, and ginger and cook for 6 minutes, or until softened. Transfer to a paper towel-lined plate and pat dry.
3. In a mixing bowl, combine the bok choy mixture, red pepper flakes, and ground pork.
4. Place a dumpling wrapper on a plate and add 1 tablespoon of the filling. Fold the wrapper in half and seal the edges with water. Repeat with the remaining wrappers and filling.
5. Grease the air fryer basket with cooking spray. Add the dumplings and cook for 12 minutes, or until golden brown.
6. While the dumplings are cooking, combine the sesame oil, rice vinegar, scallions, soy sauce, and honey in a mixing bowl.
7. Toss the cooked dumplings with the sauce and serve immediately.

SPICED PORK MEDALLIONS

PREP TIME: 10 MINUTES | COOK TIME: 30 MINUTES | SERVES 2

- 2 tablespoons low-sodium soy sauce
- 1 tablespoon chopped green onion
- 3 garlic cloves, minced
- 1 tablespoon olive oil
- 3/4 teaspoon five-spice powder
- 450g lean pork tenderloin, fat trimmed
- 1 tablespoon olive oil
- 15g water
- 15g dry white wine
- 10g chopped yellow onion
- 1/2 head green cabbage, sliced

1. In a bowl, combine the five-spice powder, olive oil, garlic, green onion, and soy sauce.
2. Add the pork to the marinade, cover, and marinate in the refrigerator for 2 hours.
3. Preheat your air fryer to 200°C (400°F).
4. Rub the pork with oil and air fry for 20-25 minutes, or until cooked through.
5. Transfer the cooked pork to a plate and keep it aside.
6. Add the wine to the same pan and place it over medium-high heat.
7. Deglaze the pan and stir in the onion. Cook for 1 minute.

8. Add the cabbage and 1 tablespoon of water. Cook for 4 minutes, or until the cabbage is wilted.
9. Slice the pork and serve with the cabbage mixture on the side.

CHINESE STEAK AND BROCCOLI

PREP TIME: 45 MINUTES | COOK TIME: 12 MINUTES | SERVES 4

- 350 grams round steak, cut into strips
- 500 grams broccoli florets
- 80 milliliters oyster sauce
- 4 teaspoons sesame oil
- 2 teaspoons soy sauce
- 2 teaspoons sugar
- 80 milliliters sherry
- 15 milliliters olive oil
- 1 garlic clove, minced

1. In a bowl, whisk together the sesame oil, oyster sauce, soy sauce, sherry, and sugar.
2. Add the beef and toss to coat.
3. Marinate the beef in the refrigerator for 30 minutes.
4. Preheat the air fryer to 190 degrees Celsius (375 degrees Fahrenheit).
5. Transfer the beef to an air fryer-safe pan. Add the broccoli, garlic, and olive oil.
6. Cook for 12 minutes, or until the beef is cooked through and the broccoli is tender.
7. Serve immediately.

STUFFED PORK CHOPS

PREP TIME: 5 MINUTES | COOK TIME: 10 MINUTES | SERVES 4

- 4 boneless pork chops (about 450 grams)
- 20 grams garlic powder
- 2 cups frozen spinach, thawed and squeezed dry
- 4 tablespoons ricotta cheese
- ¼ teaspoon sea salt
- 4 tablespoons pesto

1. Preheat the air fryer to 190 degrees Celsius.
2. Create a pocket in each pork chop by cutting a slice in the middle but not all the way through.
3. Season the inside of the chops with the garlic, then stuff each pork chop with 100 grams of spinach and 1 tablespoon of ricotta cheese. Secure the open end with a toothpick. Top each pork chop with salt and 1 tablespoon of pesto.
4. Working in batches if necessary, place the pork chops in a single layer in the air fryer basket. Cook for 5 minutes, then flip and cook for another 5 minutes, until the internal temperature reaches 63 degrees Celsius.

BEEF WELLINGTON WONTONS

PREP TIME: 35 MINUTES | COOK TIME: 10 MINUTES | SERVES 3

- 225g lean ground beef
- 1 tablespoon olive oil
- 1 1/2 teaspoons chopped shallot
- 1/4 cup dry red wine

- 1/2 teaspoon salt
- 1 package wonton wrappers (about 50)
- 1 tablespoon water
- Cooking spray
- 1 large egg, beaten
- 1/4 teaspoon pepper
- 1 tablespoon minced fresh parsley
- 1 cup each chopped fresh shiitake, baby portobello, and white mushrooms
- 2 garlic cloves, minced
- 1 tablespoon butter

1. Preheat your air fryer to 170°C/325°F.
2. In a small skillet, cook the ground beef over medium heat until no longer pink, about 4-5 minutes. Transfer to a large bowl.
3. In the same skillet, melt the butter and olive oil over medium heat. Add the garlic and shallot and cook for about 1-2 minutes. Stir in the mushrooms and wine and cook until the mushrooms are tender. Add to the beef mixture along with the parsley, salt, and pepper.
4. To make the wontons, place about 2 teaspoons of the filling in the center of each wrapper. Brush the egg and water mixture around the outside edges of each wonton. Fold opposite corners over the filling and press to seal. Place the wontons in a single layer on a tray in the air fryer basket. Spray with cooking spray.
5. Cook for 4-5 minutes, or until lightly browned. Turn the wontons and cook for an additional 4-5 minutes, or until golden brown and crisp. Serve warm or at room temperature.

BEEF STRIPS WITH SNOW PEAS AND MUSHROOMS

PREP TIME: 10 MINUTES | COOK TIME: 22 MINUTES | SERVES 2

- 2 beef steaks, cut into strips
- Salt and black pepper to taste
- 200g snow peas
- 250g white mushrooms, halved
- 1 yellow onion, cut into rings
- 4 tablespoons soy sauce
- 1 teaspoon olive oil

1. In a bowl, mix the olive oil and soy sauce. Add the beef strips and toss to coat.
2. In another bowl, combine the snow peas, onion, mushrooms, salt, pepper, and olive oil. Toss to coat.
3. Place the vegetables in a pan that fits your air fryer and cook at 175°C/350°F for 16 minutes.
4. Add the beef strips to the pan and cook at 200°C/400°F for 6 minutes more, or until the beef is cooked through.
5. Divide everything on plates and serve.
6. Enjoy!

BEEF FILLETS WITH GARLIC MAYO

PREP TIME: 10 MINUTES | COOK TIME: 40 MINUTES | SERVES 8

- 450g beef fillet
- Salt and black pepper to taste
- 100g mayonnaise
- 50g sour cream
- 2 garlic cloves, minced
- 2 tablespoons chives, chopped
- 2 tablespoons Dijon mustard
- 1/4 cup tarragon, chopped

1. Season the beef fillet with salt and pepper. Place in your air fryer and cook at 190°C for 20 minutes. Transfer to a plate and leave aside for a few minutes.
2. In a bowl, mix the garlic, sour cream, chives, mayonnaise, salt, and pepper. Whisk and leave aside.
3. In another bowl, mix the Dijon mustard and tarragon. Whisk and add the beef fillet, tossing to coat. Return to the air fryer and cook for 20 minutes more, or until the beef is cooked through.
4. Divide the beef fillet on plates and spread the garlic mayonnaise on top. Serve.

CHILI BEEF JERKY

PREP TIME: 25 MINUTES | COOK TIME: 2.5 HOURS | SERVES 6

- 400 grams (14 ounces) beef flank steak
- 1 teaspoon chili powder
- 45 milliliters (3 tablespoons) apple cider vinegar
- 1 teaspoon ground black pepper
- 1 teaspoon onion powder
- 1 teaspoon garlic powder
- 0.25 teaspoon liquid smoke

1. Cut the beef flank steak into strips about 1 centimeter (0.5 inch) thick.
2. In a bowl, combine the apple cider vinegar, ground black pepper, onion powder, garlic powder, and liquid smoke. Whisk until well combined.
3. Add the beef strips to the bowl and stir to coat.
4. Cover the bowl and refrigerate for at least 2 hours, or up to 8 hours.
5. Preheat the air fryer to 150 degrees Celsius (300 degrees Fahrenheit).
6. Line the air fryer basket with parchment paper.
7. Remove the beef strips from the marinade and place them in the air fryer basket.
8. Cook the beef jerky for 2.5 hours, or until it is dry and chewy.
9. Let the beef jerky cool completely before serving.

PORK BURGERS WITH RED CABBAGE SLAW

PREP TIME: 20 MINUTES | COOK TIME: 8 MINUTES | SERVES 4

- 125g Greek yogurt
- 4 tablespoons low-sodium mustard, divided
- 1 tablespoon lemon juice
- 1/4 cup shredded red cabbage
- 1/4 cup grated carrot
- 500g lean ground pork
- 1/2 teaspoon paprika
- 1 cup mixed salad leaves
- 2 tomatoes, sliced
- 8 wholemeal burger buns, halved

1. In a small bowl, combine 2 tablespoons of mustard, yogurt, cabbage, lemon juice, and carrot; mix and refrigerate.
2. In a medium bowl, combine the pork, paprika, and the remaining 2 tablespoons of mustard. Form into 8 small patties.
3. Place the patties in the air fryer basket. Air fry at 200 degrees Celsius (400 degrees Fahrenheit) for 8 minutes.
4. Assemble the burgers by placing a salad leaf on the bottom of a bun. Add a tomato slice, the patties, and the cabbage mixture. Add the top of the bun and serve.

PORK TRINOZA WRAPPED IN HAM

PREP TIME: 8 MINUTES | COOK TIME: 9 MINUTES | SERVES 6

- 6 pieces Serrano ham, thinly sliced
- 454 g. pork, halved, with butter and crushed
- 6 g. salt
- 1 g. black pepper
- 227 g. fresh spinach leaves, divided

- 4 slices Mozzarella cheese, divided
- 18 g. sun-dried tomatoes, divided
- 10 ml olive oil, divided

1. Place 3 pieces of ham on baking paper, slightly overlapping each other. Place 1 half of the pork in the ham. Repeat with the other half. Season the inside of the pork rolls with salt and pepper.
2. Place half of the spinach, cheese, and sun-dried tomatoes on top of the pork loin, leaving a 13 mm. border on all sides.
3. Roll the fillet around the filling and tie it with a kitchen cord to keep it closed.
4. Repeat the process for the other pork steak and place them in the fridge.
5. Warm in the air fryer and press START/PAUSE.
6. Brush the olive oil on each wrapped steak and place them in the preheated air fryer.
7. Select STEAK. Set the timer to 9 minutes and press START/PAUSE. Let it cool before cutting.

STUFFED CABBAGE AND PORK LOIN ROLLS

PREP TIME: 5 MINUTES | COOK TIME: 20 MINUTES | SERVES 4

- 500 g. white cabbage
- 1 onion
- 8 pork tenderloin steaks
- 2 carrots
- 4 tbsp. soy sauce
- 50 g. extra virgin olive oil
- Salt to taste
- 8 sheets rice

1. Put the chopped cabbage in the Thermo mix glass together with the onion and the chopped carrot.
2. Select 5 seconds on the speed 5. Add the extra virgin olive oil. Select 5 minutes, left turn, and spoon speed.
3. Cut the tenderloin steaks into thin strips. Add the meat to the thermo mix glass. Select 5 minutes, room temperature, left turn, spoon speed without beaker.
4. Add the soy sauce. Select 5 minutes, room temperature, left turn, spoon speed. Rectify salt. Let it cold down.
5. Hydrate the rice slices. Extend and distribute the filling between them.
6. Make the rolls, folding so that the edges are completely closed. Set the rolls in the air fryer and paint with the oil.
7. Select 10 minutes for cooking time and set the temperature to 190°C.

HOMEMADE FLAMINGOS

PREP TIME: 8 MINUTES | COOK TIME: 8 MINUTES | SERVES 4

- 400 g. pork fillets, very thin sliced
- 2 eggs, boiled and chopped
- 100 g. Serrano ham, chopped
- 1 egg, beaten
- 1 cup breadcrumbs

1. Make a roll with the pork fillets. Introduce half-cooked egg and Serrano ham. So that the roll does not lose its shape, fasten with a string or chopsticks.
2. Pass the rolls through the beaten egg and then through the breadcrumbs until it forms a good layer.
3. Warm the air fryer for a few minutes at 190°C. Insert the rolls in the basket and set the timer for 8 minutes.

PORK CHOPS

PREP TIME: 5 MINUTES | COOK TIME: 16 MINUTES | SERVES 4

- 4 boneless pork chops
- 2mg teaspoon caster sugar

- 1/2 teaspoon onion powder
- 5mg celery salt
- 5mg salt
- 5mg garlic powder
- 1/2 teaspoon parsley
- 1 tablespoon vegetable oil

1. Preheat your air fryer to 180°C.
2. In a small bowl, combine the caster sugar, onion powder, celery salt, salt, garlic powder, and parsley.
3. Rub the mixture all over the pork chops.
4. Drizzle the pork chops with vegetable oil.
5. Cook for 5 minutes per side for thin chops and 8 minutes per side for thick ones, or until the internal temperature reaches 74°C.

MEATBALLS WITH SAUCE

PREP TIME: 10 MINUTES | COOK TIME: 12 MINUTES | SERVES 8

- 500g ground beef
- 1 egg, beaten
- 1 cup tomato sauce
- Salt and pepper to taste
- 1 small onion, minced
- 1/2 cup breadcrumbs
- 2 carrots, grated
- 1/2 teaspoon garlic salt

1. Preheat your air fryer to 200°C.
2. In a bowl, combine the egg, carrots, breadcrumbs, onion, ground beef, garlic salt, salt, and pepper. Mix well.
3. Roll the mixture into small meatballs.
4. Place the meatballs in the air fryer basket and cook for 7 minutes.
5. Transfer the meatballs to an ovenproof dish and pour the tomato sauce over the top.
6. Place the dish in the air fryer and cook at 160°C (320°F) for 5 minutes, or until the meatballs are cooked through and the sauce is hot.

CRUMBED PORK & SEMI-DRIED TOMATO PESTO

PREP TIME: 10 MINUTES | COOK TIME: 20 MINUTES | SERVES 2

- 125ml milk
- 1 egg
- 1 cup breadcrumbs
- 1 tablespoon grated Parmesan cheese
- 1/4 bunch chopped thyme
- 1 teaspoon pine nuts
- 1/4 cup semi-dried tomatoes, chopped
- 1/2 cup almond flour
- 2 pork cutlets
- Zest of 1 lemon
- Sea salt and black pepper to taste
- 6 basil leaves
- 1 tablespoon olive oil

1. In a shallow bowl, whisk together the milk and egg. In another shallow bowl, combine the breadcrumbs, Parmesan cheese, thyme, lemon zest, salt, and pepper. In a third shallow bowl, place the almond flour. Dip each pork cutlet in the almond flour, then in the egg mixture, and then in the breadcrumb mixture.

The Complete UK Tower Air Fryer Cookbook

2. Preheat your air fryer to 180°C (360°F). Spray the air fryer basket with cooking spray. Place the pork cutlets in the air fryer basket and cook for 20 minutes, or until golden brown and cooked through.
3. While the pork is cooking, make the pesto: In a food processor, combine the semi-dried tomatoes, pine nuts, olive oil, and basil leaves. Blend until smooth.
4. Serve the pork cutlets with the pesto and a salad of your choice.

CHINESE-STYLE BEEF & BROCCOLI

PREP TIME: 10 MINUTES | COOK TIME: 12 MINUTES | SERVES 4

- 750ml oyster sauce
- 4 teaspoons sesame oil
- 1 teaspoon cornstarch
- 80ml sherry
- 2 teaspoons soy sauce
- 1 teaspoon liquid stevia
- 350g beef, cut into strips
- 500g broccoli, cut into florets
- 1 tablespoon olive oil
- 1 clove garlic, minced
- 1 slice of ginger, fresh

1. For the marinade, in a bowl, combine the oyster sauce, sesame oil, cornstarch, sherry, soy sauce, and stevia. Mix well.
2. Place the beef strips in the marinade and leave to marinate for about 1 hour.
3. Preheat your air fryer to 190°C (390°F).
4. Remove the beef from the marinade and place in the air fryer basket along with the broccoli. Drizzle with olive oil, garlic, and ginger.
5. Cook for 12 minutes, or until the beef is cooked through and the broccoli is tender.

DIET BOILED RIBS

PREP TIME: 10 MINUTES | COOK TIME: 30 MINUTES | SERVES 4

- 400 g pork ribs
- 1 tsp. black pepper
- 1 g bay leaf
- 1 tsp. basil
- 1 white onion
- 1 carrot
- 1 tsp. cumin
- 700 ml of water

1. Cut the ribs on the portions and sprinkle them with black pepper.
2. Take a big saucepan and pour water into it.
3. Add the ribs and bay leaf.
4. Peel the onion and carrot and add them to the water with meat.
5. Sprinkle it with cumin and basil. Cook it on medium heat in the air fryer for 30 minutes.

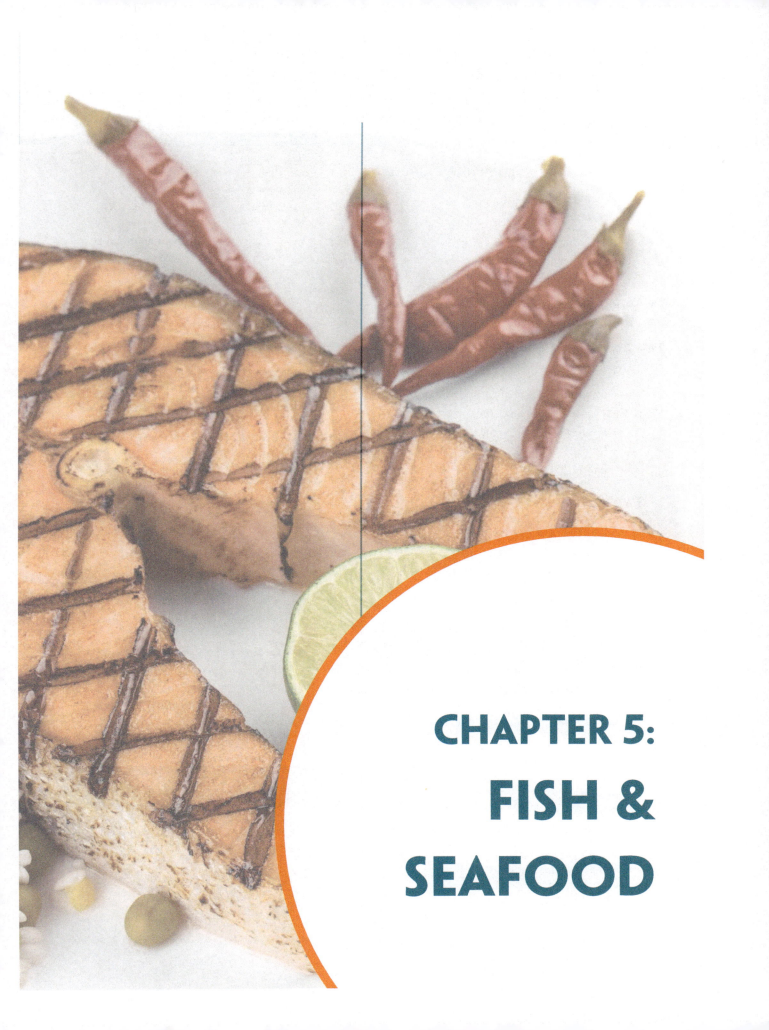

CHAPTER 5:
FISH & SEAFOOD

COCONUT SHRIMP

PREP TIME: 10 MINUTES | COOK TIME: 6 MINUTES | SERVES 6.

- 100g all-purpose flour
- 2 eggs, beaten
- 75g wholewheat breadcrumbs
- 100g unsweetened coconut flakes
- 340g peeled and deveined shrimp
- Cooking spray
- Salt, to taste
- Pepper, to taste
- 60ml lime juice
- 60ml honey
- 1 Serrano chilli, chopped (optional)

1. In a bowl, combine the flour and pepper.
2. In a separate bowl, whisk the eggs.
3. In a third bowl, combine the breadcrumbs and coconut flakes.
4. Dip the shrimp in the flour mixture, then the egg mixture, and then the breadcrumb mixture.
5. Spray the shrimp with cooking spray.
6. Air fry the shrimp for 3 minutes on each side, or until cooked through.
7. Season with salt and pepper to taste.
8. In a small bowl, combine the lime juice, honey, and Serrano chilli (if using).
9. Serve the shrimp with the honey lime dip.

GRILLED LEMON TO GLAZED SALMON

PREP TIME: 9 MINUTES | COOK TIME: 8 MINUTES | SERVES 4

- 2 tablespoons olive oil
- 2 salmon fillets
- 80ml lemon juice
- 80ml water
- 80ml gluten-free light soy sauce
- 80ml honey
- Scallions, for garnish
- Black pepper, to taste
- Garlic powder, to taste
- Kosher salt, to taste

1. Season the salmon fillets with salt, pepper, garlic powder, and kosher salt.
2. In a mixing bowl, combine the honey, soy sauce, lemon juice, water, and olive oil.
3. Place the salmon fillets in the marinade and turn to coat. Marinate for at least 2 hours, or up to overnight.
4. Preheat the air fryer to 180°C.
5. Cook the salmon fillets in the air fryer for 8 minutes, or until cooked through.
6. Garnish with scallions and serve immediately.

CHIPOTLE SPICED SHRIMP

PREP TIME: 10 MINUTES | COOK TIME: 5 MINUTES | SERVES 2

- 450g uncooked shrimp, peeled and deveined
- 2 tablespoons low-sodium tomato paste
- 3 teaspoons water
- 1/2 teaspoon olive oil
- 1/2 teaspoon minced garlic
- 5mg chipotle chili powder
- 1/2 teaspoon chopped fresh oregano

1. In a bowl, combine the tomato puree, water, olive oil, chili powder, oregano, and garlic.
2. Add the shrimp and toss to coat.
3. Cover the bowl and refrigerate for 5 minutes.
4. Preheat your air fryer to 200°C and grease it with cooking spray.
5. Air fry the shrimp for 3-4 minutes, or until pink and opaque.
6. Serve immediately.

FISH AND CHIPS

PREP TIME: 5 MINUTES | COOK TIME: 10 MINUTES | SERVES 3

- 200g frozen french fries
- 100g panko breadcrumbs
- 50g all-purpose flour

- 1/2 teaspoon garlic powder
- 1/4 teaspoon black pepper
- 1/2 teaspoon salt
- 1 teaspoon paprika
- 1 egg, beaten
- 400g cod fillets, skinned and cut into serving-size pieces

1. Preheat your air fryer to 180°C/350°F.
2. In a shallow bowl, combine the breadcrumbs, flour, garlic powder, pepper, salt, and paprika.
3. In a separate shallow bowl, whisk the egg.
4. Dip the fish fillets in the egg, then coat them in the breadcrumb mixture.
5. Place the coated fish fillets in the air fryer basket.
6. Cook for 10 minutes, or until golden brown and cooked through.
7. Serve with the french fries and your favorite dipping sauce.

SESAME SALMON KEBABS WITH ALMOND GREEN BEANS

PREP TIME: 10 MINUTES, PLUS 10 MINUTES TO MARINATE | COOK TIME: 10 MINUTES | SERVES 4

- 45 ml freshly squeezed lemon juice
- 45 ml extra-virgin olive oil, divided
- 45 ml sesame seeds, divided
- 15 ml granulated garlic
- ¼ teaspoon freshly ground black pepper
- ¼ teaspoon coconut sugar
- 340 g wild salmon, skin removed, cut into 2.5 centimeter pieces
- 2 lemons, cut into wedges
- 450 g fresh green beans
- 1 garlic clove, minced
- 30 g slivered almonds
- ¼ teaspoon sea salt

1. In a large bowl, whisk together the lemon juice, 1.5 tablespoons of olive oil, 1.5 tablespoons of sesame seeds, the granulated garlic, black pepper, and coconut sugar. Add the salmon and let marinate for 10 minutes.

2. Preheat the air fryer to 175 degrees Celsius (350 degrees Fahrenheit). If using wooden skewers, soak them in water for at least 30 minutes to prevent them from burning.
3. Thread the salmon and lemon wedges onto the skewers.
4. In a separate bowl, stir together the green beans, the remaining 1.5 tablespoons of olive oil, remaining 1.5 tablespoons of sesame seeds, minced garlic, almonds, and salt.
5. Working in batches if necessary, place the beans on the bottom of the air fryer basket in a single layer and the salmon skewers on top of the beans. Cook for 10 minutes, flipping halfway through cooking. The skewers are done when the internal temperature of the salmon reaches 63 degrees Celsius (145 degrees Fahrenheit). Be sure not to overcook them.

COD FILLET

PREP TIME: 10 MINUTES | COOK TIME: 15 MINUTES | SERVES 4

- 450g cod fillets
- 1/2 teaspoon salt
- 1/4 teaspoon black pepper
- 50g flour

- 1 large egg, beaten
- 100g panko breadcrumbs
- 1/2 teaspoon garlic powder
- 1/2 teaspoon old bay seasoning
- 1 tablespoon grated Parmesan cheese
- Olive oil spray, if needed

1. Season the cod fillets with salt and pepper.
2. In a shallow bowl, combine the flour, egg, and panko breadcrumbs.
3. Add the garlic powder, old bay seasoning, and Parmesan cheese to the breadcrumb mixture.
4. Dip each cod fillet in the egg mixture, then coat with the breadcrumb mixture.
5. Place the coated cod fillets in the air fryer basket.
6. Spray the air fryer basket with olive oil spray, if needed.
7. Cook at 180°C/350°F for 10 minutes.
8. Turn the cod fillets over and cook for an additional 3-5 minutes, or until an internal temperature of 145°F has been reached.

PARMESAN WALNUT SALMON

PREP TIME: 10 MINUTES | COOK TIME: 12 MINUTES | SERVES 4

- 4 salmon fillets
- 50g grated Parmesan cheese
- 100g walnuts
- 1 teaspoon olive oil
- 1 tablespoon lemon zest

1. Preheat your air fryer to 190°C.
2. Line an air fryer baking dish with parchment paper.
3. Place the salmon fillets in the baking dish.
4. Blitz the walnuts in a food processor until finely ground.
5. In a bowl, combine the ground walnuts, Parmesan cheese, olive oil, and lemon zest. Stir well.
6. Spoon the walnut mixture over the salmon fillets and press gently.

7. Cook in the air fryer for 12 minutes, or until the salmon is cooked through.
8. Serve and enjoy!

LEMONY AND SPICY COCONUT CRUSTED SALMON

PREP TIME: 10 MINUTES | COOK TIME: 6 MINUTES | SERVES 4

- 450g salmon fillet
- 50g plain flour
- 2 egg whites, beaten
- 50g breadcrumbs
- 50g unsweetened coconut, shredded
- 1/4 teaspoon lemon zest
- Salt
- Freshly ground black pepper
- 1/4 teaspoon cayenne pepper
- 1/4 teaspoon crushed red pepper flakes
- Vegetable oil, for greasing

1. Preheat your air fryer to 200°C. Grease an air fryer basket.
2. In a shallow dish, combine the flour, salt, and black pepper.
3. In a separate shallow dish, whisk the egg whites.
4. In a third shallow dish, combine the breadcrumbs, coconut, lemon zest, salt, cayenne pepper, and crushed red pepper flakes.
5. Dip the salmon fillet in the flour mixture, then the egg white mixture, then the breadcrumb mixture, coating evenly.
6. Place the salmon fillet in the air fryer basket and drizzle with vegetable oil.
7. Cook in the air fryer for 6 minutes, or until the salmon is cooked through.
8. Serve immediately.

SHRIMP SCAMPI

PREP TIME: 18 MINUTE | COOK TIME: 10 MINUTES | SERVES 4

- 450 grams medium shrimp, peeled and deveined
- 1/2 lemon
- 60 milliliters heavy cream
- 1 tablespoon chopped fresh parsley
- 16 grams salted butter
- 1/4 teaspoon xanthan gum
- 1/4 teaspoon red pepper flakes
- 1 teaspoon roasted garlic, minced

1. In a saucepan over medium heat, melt the butter. Zest the lemon and add it to the pan, along with the garlic.
2. Pour in the cream, xanthan gum, and red pepper flakes. Cook until the mixture begins to thicken, about 2-3 minutes.
3. Place the shrimp in a 4-cup round baking dish. Pour the cream sauce over the shrimp and cover with foil. Place the dish in the air fryer basket.
4. Preheat the air fryer to 200 degrees Celsius (400 degrees Fahrenheit) and set the timer for 8 minutes. Stir twice during cooking.
5. Garnish with parsley and serve warm.

CRAB CAKES

PREP TIME: 20 MINUTES | COOK TIME: 10 MINUTES | SERVES 4

- 1/2 medium green bell pepper, seeded and chopped
- 1/4 cup spring onion, chopped
- 1 large egg
- 200g lump crabmeat
- 1/4 cup ground almond flour
- 1/2 tablespoon lemon juice
- 2 tablespoons full-fat mayonnaise
- 1/2 teaspoon Old Bay seasoning
- 1/2 teaspoon Dijon mustard

1. In a large bowl, combine all the ingredients.
2. Shape the mixture into 4 patties.
3. Place the patties in the basket of the air fryer.
4. Preheat the air fryer to 175 degrees Celsius (350 degrees Fahrenheit).
5. Cook the patties for 10 minutes, or until golden brown, flipping halfway through cooking.
6. Serve the crab cakes warm.

CREAMY SHRIMP NACHOS

PREP TIME: 5 MINUTES | COOK TIME: 10 MINUTES | SERVES 4

- 450 grams cleaned and deveined shrimp
- 1 tablespoon olive oil
- 4 tablespoons fresh lemon juice
- 1 teaspoon paprika
- 1/4 teaspoon ground cumin
- 1/2 teaspoon shallot powder
- 1/2 teaspoon garlic powder
- Coarse sea salt and black pepper, to taste
- 1 bag (250 grams) corn tortilla chips
- 50 grams pickled jalapeño, minced
- 225 grams Pepper Jack cheese, grated
- 125 milliliters sour cream

1. In a large bowl, combine the shrimp, olive oil, lemon juice, paprika, cumin powder, shallot powder, garlic powder, salt, and pepper. Mix well.

2. Preheat the air fryer to 200 degrees Celsius (400 degrees Fahrenheit).
3. Line the air fryer basket with aluminum foil. Spread the tortilla chips in the basket.
4. Top the tortilla chips with the shrimp mixture, jalapeño, and cheese.
5. Cook for 2 minutes, or until the cheese has melted.
6. Serve garnished with sour cream.

PEPPERY AND LEMONY HADDOCK

PREP TIME: 5 MINUTES | COOK TIME: 15 MINUTES | SERVES 4

- 100g breadcrumbs
- 2 tablespoons lemon juice
- 1/2 teaspoon black pepper
- 1/4 cup dry potato flakes
- 1 large egg, beaten
- 50g Parmesan cheese, grated
- 3 tablespoons flour
- 1/4 teaspoon salt
- 4 cod fillets

1. In a small bowl, combine the flour, black pepper, and salt.
2. In a separate bowl, combine the lemon juice, breadcrumbs, potato flakes, and Parmesan cheese.
3. Dip each cod fillet in the flour mixture, then in the egg, and then in the breadcrumb mixture.
4. Place the coated cod fillets on a baking sheet lined with parchment paper.
5. Preheat the air fryer to 190 degrees Celsius.
6. Cook the cod fillets for 15 minutes, or until cooked through.

BLACK COD WITH GRAPES, PECANS, FENNEL & KALE

PREP TIME: 10 MINUTES | COOK TIME: 15 MINUTES | SERVES 2

- 2 fillets of black cod (200g each)
- 750g kale, finely chopped
- 2 teaspoons white balsamic vinegar
- 100g pecans, chopped
- 1 cup grapes, halved
- 1 small bulb fennel, sliced into 1cm thick slices
- 4 tablespoons extra-virgin olive oil
- Salt and black pepper to taste

1. Preheat your air fryer to 200°C (400°F). Season the fish fillets with salt and pepper. Drizzle with 1 teaspoon of olive oil.
2. Place the fish in the air fryer basket, skin-side down, and cook for 10 minutes. Remove the fish from the air fryer and cover loosely with aluminum foil.
3. Combine the fennel, pecans, and grapes in a bowl. Drizzle with 2 tablespoons of olive oil and season with salt and pepper. Add to the air fryer basket and cook for an additional 5 minutes.
4. In a separate bowl, combine the kale and balsamic vinegar. Drizzle with the remaining 1 tablespoon of olive oil and toss gently.
5. Serve the fish with the kale salad and enjoy!

SWEET MUSTARD COCONUT SHRIMP

PREP TIME: 10 MINUTES | COOK TIME: 20 MINUTES | SERVES 2

- 100g breadcrumbs
- Salt and black pepper to taste
- 100g unsweetened shredded coconut
- 1/2 teaspoon cayenne pepper
- 250ml coconut milk
- 8 large shrimp, peeled and deveined
- 1 tablespoon sugar-free syrup
- 1/4 teaspoon hot sauce
- 125g orange jam, sugar-free
- 1 teaspoon mustard

GRILLED SALMON FILLETS

1. Preheat your air fryer to 175°C (350°F).
2. Place the breadcrumbs, coconut, salt, pepper, and cayenne pepper in a bowl and mix well.
3. Dip the shrimp in the coconut milk first, then in the breadcrumb mixture.
4. Line a baking sheet with parchment paper and arrange the shrimp on it.
5. Place in the air fryer and cook for 20 minutes, or until the shrimp are cooked through and the breadcrumbs are golden brown.
6. While the shrimp are cooking, whisk together the orange jam, mustard, syrup, and hot sauce.
7. Serve the shrimp immediately with the sauce drizzled over them.

CRUNCHY FISH TACO

PREP TIME: 10 MINUTES | COOK TIME: 13 MINUTES | SERVES 4

- 350g cod fillet
- Salt and black pepper to taste
- 250g tempura butter
- 250g breadcrumbs
- 125g guacamole
- 6 flour tortillas
- 50g chopped fresh cilantro
- 125g salsa
- 1 lemon, juiced

1. Cut the cod fillet lengthwise into 2-inch pieces and season with salt and pepper. Dip each cod strip in the tempura butter, then into the breadcrumbs.
2. Preheat your air fryer to 170°C (340°F) and cook the cod for 13 minutes, or until cooked through.
3. Spread the guacamole on each tortilla.
4. Place a cod stick on each tortilla and top with the cilantro, salsa, and lemon juice.
5. Fold the tortillas and serve.

PREP TIME: 10 MINUTES | COOK TIME: 8 MINUTES | SERVES 2

- 2 salmon fillets (200g each)
- 2 tablespoons olive oil
- 1 teaspoon liquid sweetener
- 80ml light soy sauce
- 80ml water
- Salt and black pepper to taste

1. Season the salmon fillets with salt and pepper.
2. Whisk together the olive oil, sweetener, soy sauce, water, and salt and pepper in a bowl.
3. Place the salmon fillets in the bowl and turn to coat in the marinade.
4. Cover the bowl and refrigerate for 2 hours.
5. Preheat your air fryer to 180°C (355°F).
6. Drain the salmon fillets and pat dry.
7. Place the salmon fillets in the air fryer basket and cook for 8 minutes, or until cooked through.
8. Serve immediately.

CHAPTER 6: SIDE DISHES AND SNACKS

CHIPS WITH GARLIC AND KALE

PREP TIME: 67 MINUTES | COOK TIME: 5 MINUTES | SERVES 2

- 15g nutritional yeast flakes
- Sea salt, to taste
- 400g kale, packed
- 2 tablespoons olive oil
- 1 teaspoon minced garlic
- 1/2 cup ranch seasoning mix

1. Preheat the air fryer to 190°C.
2. In a mixing bowl, combine the olive oil, kale, garlic, and ranch seasoning.
3. Stir in the nutritional yeast flakes.
4. Spread the kale mixture in the air fryer basket.
5. Cook for 5 minutes, or until the kale is crispy.
6. Shake the basket and cook for a further 3 minutes, or until the kale is cooked through.
7. Serve immediately.

BALLS OF SALMON AND GARLIC

PREP TIME: 67 MINUTES | COOK TIME: 10 MINUTES | SERVES 2

- 170g canned salmon, drained and flaked
- 1 large egg
- 3 tablespoons olive oil
- 5 tablespoons wheat germ
- 1/2 teaspoon garlic powder
- 1 tablespoon chopped fresh dill
- 2 tablespoons chopped spring onion
- 2 tablespoons diced celery

1. Preheat your air fryer to 190°C.
2. In a large mixing bowl, combine the salmon, egg, celery, onion, dill, and garlic.
3. Roll the mixture into golf ball-sized balls.
4. Heat the olive oil in a small saucepan over medium-low heat. Add the salmon balls and flatten them slightly.
5. Place the salmon cakes in the air fryer and cook for 10 minutes, or until golden brown and cooked through.

STEW WITH MUSHROOMS

PREP TIME: 7 MINUTES | COOK TIME: 1 HOUR AND 22 MINUTES | SERVES 3

- 450g boneless, skinless chicken breast, cut into cubes
- 2 tablespoons canola oil
- 450g sliced fresh mushrooms
- 1 tablespoon dried thyme
- 60ml water
- 4 tablespoons tomato paste
- 4 cloves garlic, minced
- 150g chopped green pepper
- 750g thinly sliced zucchini
- 1 large onion, sliced
- 1 teaspoon basil
- 1 tablespoon fresh marjoram
- 1 tablespoon dried oregano

1. Preheat the air fryer to 180°C.
2. Cut the chicken into cubes and place them in the air fryer basket. Drizzle with the canola oil.
3. Combine the mushrooms, zucchini, onion, and green pepper in a mixing bowl.
4. Add the tomato paste, water, and spices to the mushroom mixture.
5. Pour the mushroom mixture over the chicken in the air fryer basket.
6. Cook for 50 minutes, or until the chicken is cooked through.
7. Increase the heat to 170°C and cook for a further 20 minutes, or until the vegetables are tender.
8. Remove the stew from the air fryer and transfer to a large pan. Pour in some water and cook for 10 minutes, or until the stew has thickened.
9. Serve immediately.

CRISPY BEANS

PREP TIME: 10 MINUTES | COOK TIME: 20 MINUTES | SERVES 4

- 2 x 400g cans (15 oz.) of unsalted chickpeas, drained and rinsed
- 1/2 teaspoon black pepper

- 1 teaspoon garlic powder
- 1 teaspoon onion powder
- 1 teaspoon dried parsley flakes
- 2 teaspoons dried dill
- Cooking spray

1. Preheat your air fryer to 200°C.
2. In a small bowl, combine the dill, parsley, onion powder, garlic powder, and black pepper.
3. Lightly grease an air fryer basket with cooking spray.
4. Spread the chickpeas in the air fryer basket and spray with cooking spray.
5. Drizzle the spice mixture over the chickpeas and shake to coat evenly.
6. Air fry the chickpeas for 20 minutes, shaking every 5 minutes.
7. Allow the chickpeas to cool, then serve.

AIR FRYER ZUCCHINI CHIPS

PREP TIME: 10 MINUTES | COOK TIME: 10 MINUTES | SERVES 2

- 3 tablespoons Parmesan cheese, grated
- ¼ teaspoon garlic powder
- 1 courgette (zucchini), sliced into thin rounds
- 70 grams cornflour (cornstarch)
- ¼ teaspoon onion powder
- ¼ teaspoon salt
- 70 grams (¼ cup) wholemeal breadcrumbs
- 1 egg, beaten

1. Preheat the air fryer to 190 degrees Celsius.
2. In a food processor, combine the Parmesan cheese, garlic powder, breadcrumbs, onion powder, and salt. Pulse until well combined.
3. In a shallow bowl, add the cornflour.
4. In another shallow bowl, whisk the egg.
5. In a third shallow bowl, add the breadcrumb mixture.
6. Dip each courgette round in the cornflour, then the egg, and then the breadcrumb mixture.
7. Spray the air fryer basket with olive oil.
8. Add the coated courgette rounds in a single layer to the air fryer basket.
9. Air fry for 10 minutes, or until golden brown and crispy.

MINI-MEATBALLS

PREP TIME: 10 MINUTES | COOK TIME: 25 MINUTES | SERVES 6

- 500g lean ground pork
- 2 tablespoons chopped fresh cilantro
- 3 tablespoons lime juice
- 5cm piece (2 inches) ginger, grated
- 1 carrot, shredded
- Black pepper, to taste

1. Preheat your air fryer to 190°C.
2. Line a suitable baking dish with parchment paper.
3. In a bowl, combine the pork, cilantro, lime juice, ginger, carrot, and black pepper. Mix well.
4. Form the mixture into 1.5-inch round balls and place them in the baking dish.
5. Air fry the meatballs for 20-25 minutes, or until cooked through.

6. Insert a toothpick into each meatball.
7. Serve.

BACON WRAPPED AVOCADO WEDGES

PREP TIME: 30 MINUTES | COOK TIME: 30 MINUTES | SERVES 1

- 12 bacon strips
- 2 medium ripe avocados

Sauce:
- 100g mayonnaise
- 50ml lime juice
- 2-3 tablespoons sriracha chili sauce
- 1 teaspoon grated lime zest

1. Preheat your air fryer to 200°C.
2. To prepare the avocado, remove the pit and peel it.
3. Cut each half into thirds. Wrap 1 rasher of bacon around each avocado wedge.
4. Working in batches if needed, place the wedges in a single layer on a tray in the air fryer basket and then cook until the bacon is cooked for 10-15 minutes.
5. Meanwhile, stir together the mayonnaise, sriracha sauce, lime juice, and zest.
6. Serve the avocado wedges with the sauce on the side.

HERB AND LEMON CAULIFLOWER

PREP TIME: 20 MINUTES | COOK TIME: 5 MINUTES | SERVES 2

- 1 tablespoon lemon juice
- 10ml olive oil, divided
- 1/8 teaspoon crushed red pepper flakes
- 10ml minced fresh parsley
- ½ medium head cauliflower, cut into florets
- ½ tablespoon minced fresh rosemary
- 2mg salt
- ½ tablespoon minced fresh thyme
- ½ teaspoon grated lemon zest

1. Preheat your air fryer to 180°C.
2. In a large bowl, toss the cauliflower florets with 2 tablespoons of the olive oil.
3. Spread the cauliflower in a single layer in the air fryer basket.
4. Cook for 8-10 minutes, or until tender and the edges are browned, stirring halfway through.
5. In a small bowl, combine the lemon juice, remaining 2 tablespoons olive oil, red pepper flakes, parsley, rosemary, salt, thyme, and lemon zest.
6. Drizzle the herb mixture over the cooked cauliflower and toss to combine.

BREADED SUMMER SQUASH

PREP TIME: 15 MINUTES | COOK TIME: 10 MINUTES | SERVES 2

- 100g grated Parmesan cheese
- 2 tablespoons olive oil
- 2 cups thinly sliced yellow summer squash
- 1/4 teaspoon salt
- 50g panko breadcrumbs
- 1/4 teaspoon black pepper
- 1/8 teaspoon cayenne pepper

1. Preheat your air fryer to 175°C.
2. In a large bowl, mix the squash and oil. Season with salt, pepper, and cayenne pepper.
3. Coat both sides of the squash in breadcrumbs and cheese. Pat to help the coating adhere.
4. Arrange the slices of squash in a single layer on a tray in your air fryer basket.
5. Cook until the squash is tender and golden brown, about 10 minutes.

CHEWY DATE BARS

PREP TIME: 10 MINUTES | COOK TIME: 10 MINUTES | MAKES 4 BARS

- 100 g raw cashews
- 50 g unsalted natural peanut butter
- 75 g gluten-free old-fashioned rolled oats
- 30 g chia seeds
- 80 g medjool dates, pitted
- 30 ml almond milk
- 1 teaspoon ground cinnamon
- 1/2 teaspoon ground nutmeg
- 1/4 teaspoon ground cloves
- 1/8 teaspoon sea salt

1. In a high-speed blender or food processor, combine the cashews, peanut butter, oats, chia seeds, dates, almond milk, cinnamon, nutmeg, cloves, and salt. Pulse on high speed until the ingredients are well combined and the dough starts to come together.
2. Line the air fryer basket or an air fryer baking pan with parchment paper. Pour the batter into the bottom, pressing it firmly down with your fingers to form an even layer. Set the temperature to 160 degrees Celsius (320 degrees Fahrenheit) and cook for 8 minutes, until golden brown on top.
3. Allow to cool completely, then cut into 2-inch-thick bars.

GARLIC-ROSEMARY BRUSSELS SPROUTS

PREP TIME: 15 MINUTES | COOK TIME: 15 MINUTES | SERVES 2

- 250g Brussels sprouts, halved
- 1 tablespoon olive oil
- 1/2 teaspoon chopped fresh rosemary
- 1/4 teaspoon salt
- 1/8 teaspoon black pepper
- 50g panko breadcrumbs

1. Preheat your air fryer to 175°C.
2. In a small bowl, combine the olive oil, rosemary, salt, and pepper.
3. Toss the Brussels sprouts with the oil mixture.
4. Place the Brussels sprouts in the air fryer basket and cook for 4-5 minutes, stirring halfway through cooking time.
5. Stir the Brussels sprouts after they have browned so you get lots of brown spots on them.
6. Cook for about 8 minutes longer, stirring halfway through cooking time.
7. Once they are tender, toss them with the panko breadcrumbs and cook until all sides are crispy enough to eat and have golden brown color.

KALE & CELERY CRACKERS

PREP TIME: 10 MINUTES | COOK TIME: 20 MINUTES | SERVES 6

- 150 grams (1 cup) ground flaxseed
- 150 grams (1 cup) soaked flaxseed (see instructions below)
- 2 bunches kale, chopped
- 1 bunch basil, chopped
- 1/2 bunch celery, chopped
- 2 garlic cloves, minced
- 80 milliliters (1/3 cup) olive oil

1. Soak the flaxseed in water for at least 8 hours, or overnight. Drain and set aside.
2. In a food processor, combine the ground flaxseed, kale, basil, celery, garlic, and olive oil. Process until well combined.

3. Spread the mixture into the air fryer basket and break it into medium-sized crackers.
4. Cook in the air fryer for 20 minutes, or until golden brown and crispy.

CRISPY BRUSSELS SPROUTS

PREP TIME: 5 MINUTES | COOK TIME: 15 MINUTES | SERVES 4

- 200 grams (2 cups) Brussels sprouts, halved
- 50g sliced almonds
- 50g grated Parmesan cheese
- 2 tablespoons olive oil
- 1 teaspoon kosher salt
- 2 tablespoons everything bagel seasoning

1. Preheat the air fryer to 190 degrees Celsius.
2. In a large bowl, combine the Brussels sprouts, almonds, Parmesan cheese, olive oil, salt, and everything bagel seasoning. Toss to coat.
3. Spread the Brussels sprouts in the air fryer basket.
4. Cook in the air fryer for 12-15 minutes, or until golden brown and crispy.

SWEET POTATO CAULIFLOWER PATTIES

PREP TIME: 20 MINUTES | COOK TIME: 20 MINUTES | SERVES 7

- 1 large sweet potato, peeled and diced
- 1 teaspoon garlic, minced
- 200 grams cauliflower florets, chopped
- 1/4 cup chopped spring onion
- ¼ teaspoon ground black pepper
- ¼ teaspoon salt
- 100 grams (1/2 cup) sunflower seeds
- ¼ teaspoon ground cumin
- 70 grams (1/4 cup) ground flaxseed
- ½ teaspoon cayenne pepper
- 2 tablespoons ranch dressing mix
- 2 tablespoons arrowroot starch

1. Preheat the air fryer to 200 degrees Celsius (400 degrees Fahrenheit).
2. In a food processor, combine the sweet potato, garlic, cauliflower, spring onion, pepper, salt, sunflower seeds, cumin, ground flaxseed, cayenne pepper, ranch dressing mix, and arrowroot starch. Pulse until well combined.
3. Shape the mixture into 7 1 1/2-inch thick cakes.
4. Place the cakes on a baking sheet and freeze for 10 minutes.
5. Grease the air fryer basket with olive oil.
6. Add the cakes to the air fryer basket in a single layer.
7. Cook for 20 minutes, flipping the cakes halfway through.
8. Serve immediately.

CHAPTER 7:
VEGAN & VEGETARIAN

BLACK BEAN BURGERS WITH LETTUCE "BUNS"

PREP TIME: 20 MINUTES | COOK TIME: 10 MINUTES | MAKES 4 BURGERS

- 125 g uncooked brown rice
- 750 g canned low-sodium black beans, drained and rinsed
- 60 g brown rice flour
- 125 g red onion, chopped
- 250 g red bell pepper, diced
- 60 g chopped fresh cilantro
- 1 teaspoon chili powder
- 1 teaspoon freshly ground black pepper
- ¼ teaspoon sea salt
- 1 medium hass avocado, sliced
- 1 tomato, sliced
- 1 head of butter lettuce

1. Preheat the air fryer to 175 degrees Celsius (350 degrees Fahrenheit). Cook the brown rice according to the package directions.
2. Mash the black beans in a large bowl until they are broken up, leaving some whole beans visible.
3. Stir in the brown rice, rice flour, onion, bell pepper, cilantro, chili powder, black pepper, and salt until evenly combined. Transfer to the refrigerator for 5 minutes to chill so that it is easier to form into patties.
4. Divide the bean mixture into 4 patties, about 12.5 centimeters in diameter.
5. Working in batches if necessary, place the patties in a single layer in the air fryer basket and cook for 8 minutes. Flip them over and cook for another 2 minutes, or until golden brown.
6. To assemble, top each black bean patty with one-quarter of the avocado and tomato slices. Using 2 or 3 lettuce leaves per patty, wrap the leaves around the patty as tightly as you can.

ARTICHOKES AND HOT TOMATOES WITH PENNE

PREP TIME: 20 MINUTES | COOK TIME: 10 MINUTES | SERVES 4

- 340 grams chickpea penne
- 4 cups whole plum or cherry tomatoes
- 1 jar marinated artichoke hearts, drained and diced (about 140 grams)
- 30 milliliters extra-virgin olive oil
- 15 milliliters dried basil
- 15 milliliters dried oregano
- 4 grams garlic powder or granules

1. Preheat the air fryer to 190 degrees Celsius. Cook the pasta according to the package directions.
2. In a large bowl, combine the tomatoes, artichoke hearts, olive oil, basil, oregano, and garlic powder.
3. Line the air fryer basket with parchment paper. Place the tomato mixture in the basket, working in batches if necessary. Cook for 10 minutes, or until the tomatoes begin to blister and pop.
4. Once the tomatoes and artichokes are cooked, combine them with the pasta and serve immediately.

FENNEL BRAISED

PREP TIME: 10 TO 20 MINUTES | COOK TIME: 14 MINUTES | SERVES 4

- 2 trimmed and quartered fennel bulbs
- 75ml extra-virgin olive oil
- 100ml white wine (optional)
- 100g grated Parmesan cheese (optional)
- 300ml vegetable broth
- 125ml lemon juice
- 1 sliced garlic clove
- 1 tablespoon dried red pepper flakes (optional)
- Salt and black pepper, to taste

1. Preheat the air fryer to 180°C.
2. Heat the olive oil in the air fryer basket on the "Sauté" setting.
3. Add the garlic and red pepper flakes (if using) and cook for 2 minutes, or until fragrant.
4. Remove the garlic.
5. Add the fennel to the air fryer basket and cook for 8 minutes, or until softened.

6. Season with salt and pepper.
7. Add the vegetable broth and white wine (if using) to the air fryer basket.
8. Cover the air fryer basket and cook for 4 minutes, or until the fennel is tender.
9. Quick release the pressure.
10. Stir in the lemon juice, Parmesan cheese (if using), and more salt and pepper to taste.
11. Toss to coat.
12. Serve immediately.

VEGETARIAN CHILLI WITH TOFU

PREP TIME: 15 MINUTES | COOK TIME: 31 MINUTES | SERVES 4

- 1 tablespoon olive oil
- 1 small yellow onion, chopped
- 280g extra-firm tofu, cut into small pieces
- 2 x 400g cans of diced tomatoes with no salt
- 400g kidney beans, rinsed and drained
- 400g black beans, rinsed and drained
- 3 tablespoons chili powder
- 1 tablespoon oregano
- 1 tablespoon chopped fresh cilantro

1. Preheat your air fryer to 175°C.
2. Spread the tofu cubes in the air fryer basket and spray them with cooking spray.
3. Air fry the tofu for 10 minutes, or until golden brown.
4. Heat the olive oil in a large soup pot over medium heat. Add the onion and cook for 6 minutes, or until softened.
5. Stir in the oregano, chili powder, beans, and tomatoes. Bring to a boil, then reduce heat and simmer for 15 minutes.
6. Stir in the tofu and mix well.
7. Garnish with cilantro and serve warm.

SRIRACHA GOLDEN CAULIFLOWER

PREP TIME: 5 MINUTES | COOK TIME: 17 MINUTES | SERVES 4

- 60 milliliters vegan butter, melted
- 60 milliliters sriracha sauce
- 400 grams cauliflower florets
- 150 grams breadcrumbs
- 1 teaspoon salt

1. Preheat the air fryer to 190 degrees Celsius.
2. In a bowl, whisk together the vegan butter and sriracha sauce.
3. Add the cauliflower florets to the bowl and toss to coat.
4. In a separate bowl, combine the breadcrumbs and salt.
5. Dip the cauliflower florets in the breadcrumbs, coating each one well.
6. Place the cauliflower florets in the air fryer basket and cook for 17 minutes, or until golden brown and crispy.
7. Serve hot.

ROSEMARY AU GRATIN POTATOES

PREP TIME: 10 MINUTES | COOK TIME: 45 MINUTES | SERVES 4

- 1 kg potatoes, peeled and sliced into 1/8-inch rounds
- 1/2 cup sunflower kernels, soaked overnight
- 1/2 cup almonds, soaked overnight
- 300ml unsweetened almond milk
- 4 tablespoons nutritional yeast
- 1 teaspoon shallot powder
- 2 garlic cloves, minced
- 120ml water
- Kosher salt
- Ground black pepper, to taste
- 1 teaspoon cayenne pepper
- 1 tablespoon fresh rosemary

1. Preheat your air fryer to 160°C.
2. Grease a baking dish with a little oil.
3. Layer half of the potatoes in the baking dish.
4. In a food processor, combine the sunflower kernels, almonds, almond milk, nutritional yeast, shallot powder, and garlic. Blend until smooth.
5. Add the water and blend for a few seconds more.
6. Pour half of the sauce over the potatoes.
7. Repeat layers.
8. Sprinkle with salt, pepper, cayenne pepper, and rosemary.
9. Bake in the air fryer for 20 minutes, or until the potatoes are tender and the sauce is bubbly.
10. Serve warm.

CHICKPEAS & SPINACH WITH COCONUT

PREP TIME: 15 MINUTES | COOK TIME: 20 MINUTES | SERVES 4

- 15 milliliters lemon juice
- 100 grams dried tomatoes, chopped
- 1 teaspoon pepper
- 1 tablespoon ginger, minced
- 400 milliliters coconut milk
- 4 garlic cloves, minced
- 1 teaspoon salt
- 1/2 teaspoon cayenne pepper
- 1 onion, chopped
- 400 grams chickpeas, rinsed and drained
- 500 grams spinach
- 1 tablespoon olive oil

1. Preheat the air fryer to 190 degrees Celsius.
2. In a bowl, whisk together the lemon juice, dried tomatoes, pepper, ginger, coconut milk, garlic, salt, cayenne pepper, and onion.
3. Add the chickpeas and spinach to the bowl and stir to coat.
4. Pour the sauce over the chickpeas and spinach and stir in the olive oil.
5. Cook in the air fryer for 15 minutes, or until the spinach is wilted and the chickpeas are heated through.
6. Serve warm.

LEMONY FALAFEL

PREP TIME: 10 MINUTES | COOK TIME: 15 MINUTES | SERVES 8

- 1 teaspoon cumin seeds
- 1/2 teaspoon coriander seeds
- 240g chickpeas, drained and rinsed
- 1/2 teaspoon red pepper flakes
- 3 garlic cloves, crushed
- 1/4 cup chopped parsley
- 1/4 cup chopped coriander
- 1/2 onion, diced
- 1 tablespoon lemon juice
- 3 tablespoons plain flour
- 1/2 teaspoon salt
- Cooking spray

1. Toast the cumin and coriander seeds in a dry pan over medium heat for 1-2 minutes, or until fragrant.
2. Grind the toasted seeds using a mortar and pestle.
3. Put all ingredients, except for the cooking spray, in a food processor and blend until a fine consistency is achieved.

4. Use your hands to mold the mixture into falafels and spritz with the cooking spray.
5. Preheat your air fryer to 200°C.
6. Transfer the falafels to the air fryer basket in a single layer. Cook for 15-20 minutes, or until golden brown. Serve warm.

CAULIFLOWER RICE

PREP TIME: 10 MINUTES | COOK TIME: 22 MINUTES | SERVES 3

For the Tofu:
- 1 cup diced carrot
- 170 grams (6 ounces) extra-firm tofu, drained and pressed
- 1/2 cup diced white onion
- 2 tablespoons soy sauce
- 1 teaspoon turmeric

For the Cauliflower:
- 1/2 cup chopped broccoli
- 750 grams (3 cups) cauliflower rice
- 1 tablespoon minced garlic
- 1/2 cup frozen peas
- 1 tablespoon minced ginger
- 2 tablespoons soy sauce
- 1 tablespoon apple cider vinegar
- 2.5 teaspoons toasted sesame oil

1. Preheat the air fryer to 190°C.
2. Grease an air fryer pan with olive oil.
3. In a bowl, combine the tofu, carrot, onion, soy sauce, and turmeric.
4. Stir until well combined.
5. Add the tofu mixture to the air fryer pan and spread it out evenly.
6. Cook for 10 minutes, or until crispy, stirring halfway through.
7. In a separate bowl, combine the cauliflower, broccoli, garlic, peas, ginger, soy sauce, apple cider vinegar, and toasted sesame oil.
8. Stir until well combined.
9. Add the cauliflower mixture to the air fryer pan and spread it out evenly.

10. Cook for 12 minutes, or until tender, stirring halfway through.
11. Serve immediately.

CREAMED SPINACH

PREP TIME: 10 MINUTES | COOK TIME: 15 MINUTES | SERVES 2

- 100 grams (1/2 cup) chopped white onion
- 300 grams (10 ounces) frozen spinach, thawed and squeezed dry
- 1 teaspoon salt
- 1 teaspoon ground black pepper
- 2 teaspoons minced garlic
- 0.5 teaspoon ground nutmeg
- 115 grams (4 ounces) reduced-fat cream cheese, diced
- 30 grams (1/4 cup) reduced-fat Parmesan cheese

1. Preheat the air fryer to 175 degrees Celsius (350 degrees Fahrenheit).
2. Grease a 6-inch baking dish with olive oil.
3. In a large bowl, combine the spinach, onion, salt, pepper, garlic, nutmeg, cream cheese, and Parmesan cheese.
4. Stir until well combined.
5. Pour the mixture into the prepared baking dish.
6. Cook in the air fryer for 10 minutes, or until heated through and the cheese has melted.
7. Serve immediately.

AMERICAN-STYLE BRUSSELS SPROUT SALAD

PREP TIME: 35 MINUTES | COOK TIME: 15 MINUTES | SERVES 4

- 500 grams (1 pound) Brussels sprouts, trimmed and halved
- 1 apple, cored and diced
- 100 grams (0.5 cup) mozzarella cheese, crumbled
- 100 grams (0.5 cup) pomegranate seeds
- 1 small red onion, chopped
- 4 hard-boiled eggs, sliced

Dressing:
- 60 milliliters (0.25 cup) olive oil
- 30 milliliters (2 tablespoons) champagne vinegar
- 1 teaspoon Dijon mustard
- 1 teaspoon honey
- Salt and pepper, to taste

1. Preheat the air fryer to 190 °C.
2. Add the Brussels sprouts to the air fryer basket. Mist with cooking spray and cook for 15 minutes, or until tender and slightly browned. Let cool to room temperature for 15 minutes.
3. In a large bowl, combine the Brussels sprouts, apple, cheese, pomegranate seeds, and red onion.
4. In a small bowl, whisk together the olive oil, champagne vinegar, Dijon mustard, honey, salt, and pepper.
5. Pour the dressing over the salad and toss to coat.
6. Serve immediately, topped with the hard-boiled eggs.

CARROT & ZUCCHINI MUFFINS

PREP TIME: 10 MINUTES | COOK TIME: 14 MINUTES | SERVES 4

- 4 tablespoons butter, melted
- 1/4 cup carrots, grated
- 100g zucchini, grated
- 225g almond flour
- 2 tablespoons liquid stevia
- 2 teaspoons baking powder
- Pinch of salt
- 3 eggs
- 1 tablespoon yogurt
- 250ml milk

1. Preheat your air fryer to 180°C.
2. Beat the eggs, yogurt, milk, salt, baking powder, and stevia together.
3. Gradually whisk in the flour until just combined.
4. Stir in the zucchini and carrots.
5. Grease a 12-hole muffin tin with butter and pour the batter into the tins.
6. Cook for 14 minutes, or until a toothpick inserted into the center comes out clean.
7. Serve immediately.

CARROT AND OAT BALLS

PREP TIME: 25 MINUTES | COOK TIME: 15 MINUTES | SERVES 3

- 4 carrots, grated
- 150 grams (1 cup) ground rolled oats
- 1 tablespoon butter, softened
- 1 tablespoon chia seeds
- 1/2 cup chopped scallions
- 2 cloves garlic, minced
- 2 tablespoons tomato ketchup
- 1 teaspoon cayenne pepper
- 1/2 teaspoon salt
- 1/4 teaspoon black pepper
- 1/2 teaspoon ancho chili powder
- 50 grams (1/4 cup) fresh bread crumbs

1. Preheat the air fryer to 190 degrees Celsius (380 degrees Fahrenheit).
2. In a bowl, combine all the ingredients until well combined.
3. Shape the mixture into bite-sized balls.
4. Cook the balls in the air fryer for 15 minutes, shaking the basket halfway through.

CHAPTER 8:
DESSERTS

CARAMELIZED CINNAMON PEACHES WITH NUTTY VANILLA RICOTTA

PREP TIME: 5 MINUTES | COOK TIME: 10 MINUTES | SERVES 4

- 4 cups frozen peaches, thawed
- 40 grams ground cinnamon, divided
- 30 milliliters avocado olive oil cooking spray
- 100 grams part-skim ricotta cheese
- 1 milliliter pure vanilla extract
- 180 grams unsalted slivered almonds, for garnish
- 75 grams unsalted pumpkin seeds, for garnish

1. Preheat the air fryer to 200 degrees Celsius.
2. Lay the peaches on a flat surface and sprinkle with 20 grams of cinnamon.
3. Working in batches if necessary, mist the air fryer basket with the avocado oil. Arrange the peaches in a single layer in the air fryer basket and cook for 10 minutes, until they start to caramelize.
4. While the peaches are cooking, in a small bowl, stir together the ricotta cheese, vanilla, and remaining 20 grams of cinnamon.
5. When the peaches are done, transfer them to a plate. Scoop a dollop of the ricotta mixture on each serving and garnish with the almonds and pumpkin seeds. These peaches are best served warm, but leftovers can be refrigerated in an airtight container for up to 4 days.

CRUSTLESS CHEESECAKE

PREP TIME: 5 MINUTES | COOK TIME: 10 MINUTES | SERVES 2

- 450 grams cream cheese, softened
- 40 milliliters sour cream, reduced fat
- 150 grams erythritol sweetener
- 1 teaspoon unsweetened vanilla extract
- 2 large eggs
- 1/2 teaspoon lemon juice

1. Preheat the air fryer to 175 degrees Celsius. Grease the air fryer basket with olive oil.
2. Grease two 10 cm springform pans with olive oil.
3. In a bowl, whisk together the eggs, lemon juice, sweetener, and vanilla extract until smooth.
4. Whisk in the cream cheese and sour cream until blended.
5. Divide the mixture evenly between the prepared springform pans.
6. Place the springform pans in the air fryer basket and cook for 10 minutes, or until the cakes are set and a skewer inserted into the center comes out clean.
7. Let the cakes cool in the springform pans for 10 minutes before removing them.
8. Refrigerate the cakes for at least 3 hours before serving.

COCONUT ORANGE CAKE

PREP TIME: 10 MINUTES | COOK TIME: 17 MINUTES | SERVES 6

- 150g shredded coconut
- 1/4 teaspoon salt
- 1/3 teaspoon ground nutmeg
- 1/2 teaspoon baking powder
- 1 1/4 cups almond flour
- 2 eggs
- 2 tablespoons erythritol
- 115g (1 stick) unsalted butter, softened
- 2 tablespoons orange jam
- 1/3 cup coconut milk

1. Preheat your air fryer to 180°C (355°F). Grease and line a 7-inch cake tin with parchment paper.
2. In a large bowl, cream together the butter and erythritol until light and fluffy. Beat in the eggs one at a time, then stir in the nutmeg, salt, and flour.
3. Gradually add the coconut milk, then stir in the shredded coconut and orange jam.
4. Pour the batter into the prepared cake tin and bake in the air fryer for 17 minutes, or until a toothpick inserted into the centre comes out clean.
5. Let the cake cool completely in the tin before removing and slicing. Serve chilled.

FUDGE BROWNIES

PREP TIME: 15 MINUTES | COOK TIME: 20 MINUTES | SERVES 16.

- 120g melted butter
- 160g powdered sweetener
- 1/2 teaspoon vanilla extract
- 3 large eggs, at room temperature
- 100g ground almonds
- 60g unsweetened cocoa powder
- 1 tablespoon unflavored gelatin
- 1/2 teaspoon salt
- 1/2 teaspoon baking powder
- 60ml cold water

1. Grease and line an 8x8-inch square baking pan.
2. Preheat your air fryer to 165°C.
3. In a large bowl, whisk together the eggs, vanilla extract, sweetener, and melted butter until smooth.
4. In a separate bowl, whisk together the cocoa powder, almond flour, gelatin, salt, and baking powder.
5. Add the dry ingredients to the wet ingredients and whisk until just combined.
6. Stir in the cold water until smooth.
7. Pour the batter into the prepared baking pan and bake in the air fryer for 15 minutes, or until a toothpick inserted into the center comes out clean.
8. Let the brownies cool completely in the pan before cutting into squares and serving.

DATE & HAZELNUT COOKIES

PREP TIME: 10 MINUTES | COOK TIME: 20 MINUTES | SERVES 10

- 75g sugar-free maple syrup
- 75g pitted dates, chopped
- 60g hazelnuts, chopped
- 115g unsalted butter, softened
- 75g almond flour
- 75g cornflour
- 2 tablespoons erythritol for baking
- 1/2 teaspoon vanilla extract
- 1/3 teaspoon ground cinnamon
- 1/3 teaspoon ground cardamom

1. Cream together the butter and erythritol until light and fluffy. Stir in the maple syrup, dates, and hazelnuts.
2. Sift the flours into the bowl and mix until just combined. Stir in the vanilla extract, cinnamon, and cardamom.
3. Shape the dough into small balls and place them on a baking sheet. Flatten the balls with the back of a spoon.
4. Preheat your air fryer to 150°C (310°F).
5. Bake the cookies for 20 minutes, or until they are golden brown.
6. Let the cookies cool slightly before serving.

BREAD PUDDING WITH VANILLA

PREP TIME: 10 MINUTES | COOK TIME: 15 MINUTES | SERVES 4

- 3 beaten eggs
- 1 tablespoon melted coconut oil
- 1 teaspoon vanilla extract

- 600g bread cubes
- 1/2 teaspoon ground cinnamon
- 1/4 cup raisins
- 1/4 cup chocolate chips
- 1 liter milk
- 1/4 teaspoon salt
- 500ml water

1. Pour water into the air fryer's oven, followed by the trivet.
2. Add cubed bread to the baking dish.
3. In a large bowl, combine the rest of the ingredients.
4. Pour the mixture from the bowl over the bread cubes in the baking dish, and then cover the dish with aluminum foil.
5. Position the baking dish on the trivet.
6. Seal the pot with the cover and cook on the steam setting for 25 minutes.
7. Once complete, let the pressure release naturally for 10 minutes, and then quick release any remaining pressure.
8. Remove the baking dish from the saucepan with care.
9. Serve with gusto.

COCONUT PIE

PREP TIME: 5 MINUTES | COOK TIME: 45 MINUTES | SERVES 6

- 100g coconut flour
- 100g erythritol sweetener
- 100g unsweetened shredded coconut, divided
- 50g unsalted butter, melted
- 3 teaspoons unsweetened vanilla extract
- 2 large eggs
- 300ml low-fat unsweetened milk
- 50g unsweetened shredded coconut, toasted

1. Preheat your air fryer to 175°C.
2. Grease a 6-inch pie dish with a little oil.
3. In a bowl, combine the coconut flour, sweetener, 75g of the shredded coconut, butter, vanilla extract, and eggs. Whisk until smooth.
4. Pour the batter into the prepared pie dish and smooth the top.
5. Bake in the air fryer for 45 minutes, or until the pie is set and a toothpick inserted into the center comes out clean.
6. Let the pie cool completely before garnishing with the toasted coconut.

APPLE PIE ROLL

PREP TIME: 10 MINUTES | COOK TIME: 8 MINUTES | SERVES 4

- 610g 1 can apple pie filling
- 30ml lemon juice
- 1/4 teaspoon apple pie spice
- 1/8 teaspoon ground cinnamon
- 1 tablespoon all-purpose flour
- 4 filo pastry sheets

1. In a bowl, combine the apple pie filling, lemon juice, apple pie spice, cinnamon, and flour.
2. Spread a filo pastry sheet on a working surface in a diamond shape position.
3. Add 1/4 of the apple pie filling to one corner of the wrapper.
4. Fold the top and bottom of the wrapper and roll it neatly.
5. Wet the edges and press to seal the roll.
6. Repeat steps 2-5 with the remaining filo pastry sheets and apple pie filling.
7. Place the rolls in the air fryer basket and spray with cooking spray.
8. Preheat your air fryer to 200°C.
9. Air fry the apple pie rolls for 8 minutes in the preheated air fryer.
10. Serve warm.

CHEWY WHITE CHOCOLATE COOKIES

PREP TIME: 10 MINUTES | COOK TIME: 11 MINUTES | SERVES 10

- 2 large eggs, beaten
- 225g white chocolate, chopped
- 1/4 teaspoon fine sea salt
- 1/3 teaspoon ground nutmeg
- 1/3 teaspoon ground allspice
- 1/3 teaspoon ground anise
- 2 tablespoons erythritol
- 100g quick-cooking oats
- 2 1/4 cups almond flour
- 175g (3/4 cup) unsalted butter, softened

1. In a large bowl, combine all the ingredients, except the egg wash. Knead with your hands until a soft dough forms.
2. Place the dough in the fridge for 20 minutes.
3. Preheat your air fryer to 175°C (350°F).
4. Roll the chilled dough into small balls and flatten them in a baking pan.
5. Make an egg wash by whisking together the remaining egg. Brush the egg wash over the cookies.
6. Bake in the air fryer for 11 minutes, or until the cookies are golden brown.
7. Let the cookies cool slightly before serving.

BLACK BEAN BROWNIE

PREP TIME: 15 MINUTES | COOK TIME: 15 MINUTES | SERVES 8

- 150g canned (no salt) black beans, drained, rinsed
- 4 tablespoons cocoa powder
- 100g quick oats
- 1/4 teaspoon salt
- 80ml pure maple syrup
- 4 tablespoons sugar
- 60g coconut oil, melted
- 2 teaspoons pure vanilla extract
- 1/2 teaspoon baking powder
- 70-90g chocolate chips
- Powdered sugar, for garnish

1. Preheat your air fryer to 175°C.
2. In a blender, combine the black beans, chocolate chips, cocoa powder, oats, salt, maple syrup, sugar, oil, vanilla, and baking powder. Blend until smooth.
3. Grease an 8x8 inch pan with oil and spread the brownie dough into the pan.
4. Air fry the brownies for 15 minutes, or until a toothpick inserted into the center comes out clean.
5. Allow the brownies to cool completely before cutting into squares and garnishing with powdered sugar.
6. Serve.

BREAD PUDDING WITH SULTANAS

PREP TIME: 10 MINUTES | COOK TIME: 25 MINUTES | SERVES 8

- 1 teaspoon vanilla extract
- 1.5 tablespoons coffee liqueur
- 1 loaf stale ciabatta bread, torn into pieces
- 75g white chocolate chunks
- 3 large eggs, whisked
- 1/4 cup sultanas
- 375ml semi-skimmed milk
- 2 tablespoons erythritol for baking

1. Prepare two mixing bowls. Add the bread pieces to the first bowl.
2. In the second bowl, whisk together the remaining ingredients, except the white chocolate and sultanas.
3. Pour the egg/milk mixture over the bread pieces. Allow to soak for 20 minutes, gently pressing down with a large spatula every 5 minutes.
4. Scatter the white chocolate chunks and sultanas over the top. Divide the bread pudding between two mini loaf pans.
5. Preheat your air fryer to 160°C (320°F).
6. Bake in the air fryer for 25 minutes, or until the bread pudding is set.
7. Let the bread pudding cool slightly before serving.

CHURROS

PREP TIME: 15 MINUTES | COOK TIME: 25 MINUTES | SERVES 6

- 250ml water
- 115g unsalted butter
- 100g packed light brown sugar
- 1/2 teaspoon salt
- 225g all-purpose flour
- 2 large eggs
- 1 teaspoon vanilla extract
- 3 tablespoons granulated sugar
- 1/2 teaspoon ground cinnamon
- Confectioners' sugar, for garnish

1. Preheat your air fryer to 175°C.
2. Line a rimmed baking sheet with parchment paper.
3. In a saucepan, combine the water, butter, brown sugar, and salt. Bring to a boil, then remove from the heat and allow to cool slightly.
4. Beat in the eggs, vanilla, sugar, cinnamon, and flour until smooth.
5. Transfer the batter to a piping bag fitted with a star-tip.
6. Pipe the batter into 4-6 inch churros onto the rimmed baking sheet.
7. Refrigerate for 15 minutes to set.
8. Transfer the churros and the parchment paper to the air fryer basket in batches and air fry for 15 minutes, or until golden brown.
9. Garnish with confectioners' sugar.
10. Serve warm.

AIR-FRYER SCONES

PREP TIME: 10 MINUTES | COOK TIME: 7 MINUTES | SERVES 6

- 225g self raising flour
- 28g caster sugar
- egg wash
- squirty cream
- strawberry jam
- 50g butter
- 60 ml whole milk
- extra virgin olive oil spray
- fresh strawberries

1. Make your scones by combining flour and sugar in a bowl. Add cubed butter and rub it into the flour until it resembles coarse breadcrumbs.
2. Add enough milk to make a soft dough about 60ml.
3. Then roll out your dough on a floured worktop and make sure they are not small. Use cutters to cut your scones into medium-sized portions, then place them in the air fryer basket with a light coating of extra virgin olive oil sprayed on top to prevent them from sticking against each other.
4. Brush each side of the scones with egg wash as well as their tops and sides to give them a nice golden colour before putting them in your air fryer set at 180°C for 5 minutes followed by another 2 minutes at 160°C after they have been cooked through completely.
5. Serve with strawberry jam, sliced strawberries, cream, and plenty of orange zest!

APPENDIX 1

MEASUREMENT CONVERSION CHART

VOLUME EQUIVALENTS(DRY)

US STANDARD	METRIC (APPROXIMATE)
1/8 teaspoon	0.5 mL
1/4 teaspoon	1 mL
1/2 teaspoon	2 mL
3/4 teaspoon	4 mL
1 teaspoon	5 mL
1 tablespoon	15 mL
1/4 cup	59 mL
1/2 cup	118 mL
3/4 cup	177 mL
1 cup	235 mL
2 cups	475 mL
3 cups	700 mL
4 cups	1 L

VOLUME EQUIVALENTS(LIQUID)

US STANDARD	US STANDARD (OUNCES)	METRIC (APPROXIMATE)
2 tablespoons	1 fl.oz.	30 mL
1/4 cup	2 fl.oz.	60 mL
1/2 cup	4 fl.oz.	120 mL
1 cup	8 fl.oz.	240 mL
1 1/2 cup	12 fl.oz.	355 mL
2 cups or 1 pint	16 fl.oz.	475 mL
4 cups or 1 quart	32 fl.oz.	1 L
1 gallon	128 fl.oz.	4 L

TEMPERATURES EQUIVALENTS

FAHRENHEIT(F)	CELSIUS(C) (APPROXIMATE)
225 °F	107 °C
250 °F	120 °C
275 °F	135 °C
300 °F	150 °C
325 °F	160 °C
350 °F	180 °C
375 °F	190 °C
400 °F	205 °C
425 °F	220 °C
450 °F	235 °C
475 °F	245 °C
500 °F	260 °C

WEIGHT EQUIVALENTS

US STANDARD	METRIC (APPROXIMATE)
1 ounce	28 g
2 ounces	57 g
5 ounces	142 g
10 ounces	284 g
15 ounces	425 g
16 ounces (1 pound)	455 g
1.5 pounds	680 g
2 pounds	907 g

APPENDIX 2

The Dirty Dozen and Clean Fifteen

The Environmental Working Group (EWG) is a nonprofit, nonpartisan organization dedicated to protecting human health and the environment Its mission is to empower people to live healthier lives in a healthier environment. This organization publishes an annual list of the twelve kinds of produce, in sequence, that have the highest amount of pesticide residue-the Dirty Dozen-as well as a list of the fifteen kinds ofproduce that have the least amount of pesticide residue-the Clean Fifteen.

THE DIRTY DOZEN

- The 2016 Dirty Dozen includes the following produce. These are considered among the year's most important produce to buy organic:

Strawberries	Spinach
Apples	Tomatoes
Nectarines	Bell peppers
Peaches	Cherry tomatoes
Celery	Cucumbers
Grapes	Kale/collard greens
Cherries	Hot peppers

- The Dirty Dozen list contains two additional itemskale/collard greens and hot peppers-because they tend to contain trace levels of highly hazardous pesticides.

THE CLEAN FIFTEEN

- The least critical to buy organically are the Clean Fifteen list. The following are on the 2016 list:

Avocados	Papayas
Corn	Kiw
Pineapples	Eggplant
Cabbage	Honeydew
Sweet peas	Grapefruit
Onions	Cantaloupe
Asparagus	Cauliflower
Mangos	

- Some of the sweet corn sold in the United States are made from genetically engineered (GE) seedstock. Buy organic varieties of these crops to avoid GE produce.

APPENDIX 3: INDEX

A
active dry yeast   24
active yeast   25
agave syrup   16
all-purpose flour   12, 31, 44, 67, 69
almond butter   63
almond flour   12, 13, 14, 25, 41, 62, 63, 65, 66, 68, 69
almond milk   54
almonds   13, 21, 60
Amaretto liqueur   70
apple   62
apple cider vinegar   39, 61
apple pie filling   67
apple pie spice   67
arrowroot starch   55
asparagus spears   55
avocado   55
avocado oil   20
avocado oil cooking spray   19
avocado olive oil cooking spray   65

B
baby portobello   38
bacon   20, 25
bacon, halved lengthways   32
bacon strips   53
bagel seasoning   55
baking apples   63
baking powder   12, 22, 62, 65, 66, 68, 69
baking soda   63
balsamic vinegar   23, 28
bananas   16
basil   14, 33, 42, 51, 54
basil leaves   15, 16, 17, 34, 41
bay leaf   42
bean sprouts   17
beaten   13, 14, 22, 24, 31, 32
beef   42
beef fillet   38
beef flank steak   39
beef steaks   38
bell pepper   21
bell peppers   34
berries   20
black beans   59, 68
black cod   48
black pepper   10, 14, 17, 23, 28, 29, 30, 32, 36, 38, 39, 41, 42, 45, 47, 48, 49, 51, 53, 54, 55, 58, 61, 63
Black pepper   33, 44, 52
blanched slivered almonds   69
blueberries   22
boiling water   62
bok choy   36
bone-in, skin-on chicken thighs   32
boneless pork chops   37, 40
boneless, skinless chicken breast   29, 51
boneless, skinless chicken breast cutlets   30
boneless, skinless chicken breast fillet   28
boneless, skinless chicken thighs, cubed   31
bread   14
breadcrumbs   29, 32, 40, 41, 46, 48, 49, 59
bread cubes   67
brie cheese   14
broccoli   42, 61
broccoli florets   10, 14, 28, 37
brown rice flour   58
brown sugar   24, 28
Brussels sprouts   54, 55, 62
Buffalo sauce   56
bulb fennel   48
butter   10, 11, 21, 23, 25, 33, 38, 62, 63, 69, 70
butter-flavored cooking spray   29

butter, softened   32
button mushrooms   11

C
canned   20
canned low-sodium black beans   58
canned low-sodium chickpeas   26
canned salmon   51
canola oil   51
carrot   11, 42, 52, 61
carrots   14, 17, 40, 41, 62, 63
cashews   13
caster sugar   70
cauliflower   23
cauliflower florets   11, 55, 59
cauliflower rice   61
cayenne pepper   11, 13, 19, 33, 46, 48, 53, 55, 60, 63
celery   54
celery salt   41
Celery sticks   33
champagne vinegar   62
cheddar cheese   14, 19, 20, 21, 24, 25, 28
cherry tomatoes   19, 58
chia seeds   21, 54, 63
chicken breast   32
chicken breasts   34
chicken broth   28, 33
chicken fillet   23
chicken wings   33, 56
chickpea penne   58
chickpeas   14, 16, 60
chili powder   14, 16, 39, 58, 59, 63
chipotle chili powder   44
chips   14
chives   34, 38
chocolate chips   67, 68
chopped   10, 11, 14, 16, 17, 19, 22, 23, 28, 41
chopped bacon   25
chopped broccoli   28
chopped broccoli florets   19
chopped carrots   28
chopped cold butter   12
chopped fresh cilantro   52
Chopped fresh parsley   26
chopped fresh rosemary   30
chopped fresh shiitake   38
chopped fresh strawberries   12
chopped in a food processor   13
chopped Italian parsley   30
chopped scallions   36
chopped shallot   37
chopped thyme   41
cilantro   25
cilantro leaves   10, 16
cinnamon powder   26
cinnamon swirl bread   22
cleaned and deveined shrimp   47
clove garlic   42
cloves garlic   51
coarse sea salt   11
Coarse sea salt   47
cocoa powder   68
coconut flour   67
coconut milk   16, 20, 22, 24, 48, 60, 65
coconut oil   22, 25, 68
coconut sugar   20, 45
cod fillet   49
cod fillets   45, 48
coffee liqueur   68
cold water   62, 66
Confectioners' sugar   69
cooked   19, 25
cooked bacon   33

cooked crab meat   14
Cooking spray   19, 20, 24, 29, 36, 38, 44, 52, 60
coriander   14, 60
coriander powder   31
coriander seeds   60
Corn Chex cereal   69
cornflakes   29
cornflour   52, 66
cornstarch   42
corn tortilla chips   47
cottage cheese   23
Cottage cheese   10
courgette   14, 34, 52
cranberries   22
cream   23
cream cheese   31, 65, 70
crème fraiche   11
crescent dough   21
crumbled   11, 21, 22
crumbled low-sodium breakfast sausage   19
crushed   10, 12, 15
crushed red pepper flakes   46
cubed   14
cubed butternut squash   19
cucumber   25
cumin   42
cumin seeds   60
curry powder   16
cut into slices   12
cutlets   41

D
dark turkey meat   30
dates   26
deveined shrimp   44
diced   14, 16, 17, 23, 25, 31, 33
diced celery   51
Dijon mustard   36, 38, 47, 62
divided   11
double cream   14
drained   14, 26
dried basil   58
dried berries   21
dried breadcrumbs   30
dried dill   52
dried dill weed   10
dried fenugreek leaves   31
dried marjoram   10
dried oregano   16, 19, 20, 51, 58
dried parsley   36
dried parsley flakes   52
dried red pepper flakes   58
dried rosemary   10
dried thyme   36, 51
dried tomatoes   60
dried yeast   31
dry potato flakes   48
dry quinoa   26
dry red wine   37
dry white wine   36
dumpling wrappers   36

E
egg   12, 15, 24, 25, 29, 30, 31, 33, 38, 40, 41, 45, 46, 47, 48, 51, 52, 70
egg noodles   28
eggs   10, 11, 12, 13, 14, 15, 19, 21, 22, 23, 24, 32, 40, 44, 62, 65, 66, 67, 68, 69
egg wash   70
egg white   13
egg whites   19, 46
egg yolk   31
erythritol   65, 68
erythritol for baking   66

erythritol sweetener 65, 67
extra-firm tofu 59, 61
extra virgin olive oil 40
extra-virgin olive oil 26, 30, 45, 48, 58
extra virgin olive oil spray 70

F
fennel bulbs 58
feta cheese 22
finely chopped 10
finely chopped cooked turkey 29
finely diced 19
finely milled 22
fine sea salt 11, 68
five-spice powder 36
flaky pastry 21
flaxseed meal 20
flour 45, 48
flour tortillas 49
French bread 56
french fries 44
Fresh basil leaves 32
fresh bread crumbs 63
fresh cilantro 49, 58, 59
fresh dill 51
fresh flat-leaf parsley 30
fresh ginger 11
fresh green beans 45
fresh lemon juice 47
freshly ground black pepper 19, 30, 45, 58
Freshly ground black pepper 32, 46
freshly squeezed lemon juice 45
fresh marjoram 51
fresh mushrooms 51
fresh oregano 44
fresh parsley 47
fresh rosemary 28, 54, 60
fresh spinach 19, 22
fresh spinach leaves 39
fresh strawberries 70
fries 17
frozen peas 61
frozen spinach 37, 61
full-fat mayonnaise 47

G
garam masala 31
garlic 13, 16, 55, 63
garlic clove 19, 28, 37, 45, 58
garlic cloves 11, 16, 26, 30, 36, 38, 54, 60
garlic paste 11
garlic powder 10, 15, 28, 29, 33, 37, 39, 41, 45, 46, 47, 51, 52, 55, 56, 58
Garlic powder 44
garlic puree 14
garlic salt 41
ginger 28, 36, 52, 60
gluten-free light soy sauce 44
gluten-free old-fashioned rolled oats 54
granulated garlic 45
granulated sugar 12, 69, 70
granules 58
grapes 48
grape tomatoes 56
grated 10, 11, 13, 14, 20, 21, 24
grated carrot 39
grated cheddar cheese 21, 33
grated ginger 31
grated lemon zest 53
grated lime zest 53
grated mozzarella cheese 33
greasing 22
Greek yogurt 31, 39
green beans 16
green bell pepper 31, 47
green cabbage 36
green onion 19, 36
green onions 10
green pepper 22, 23, 51
ground allspice 68
ground almond flour 47

ground almonds 66
ground anise 68
ground beef 25, 41
ground black pepper 11, 20, 23, 25, 39, 55
Ground black pepper 10, 32, 60
ground cardamom 66
ground chicken breast 26
ground cinnamon 13, 20, 23, 54, 65, 66, 67, 69
ground cloves 13, 54
ground cumin 47, 55
ground flaxseed 25, 54, 55
ground ginger 23
ground nutmeg 23, 54, 61, 65, 68
ground rolled oats 63
ground thyme 20, 25
ground turmeric 31
guacamole 49
gyoza wrappers 11

H
halved 10, 14, 24
hard-boiled eggs 62
hass avocado 58
hazelnuts 66
head cauliflower 13, 53
head of butter lettuce 58
heavy cream 32, 47
honey 21, 34, 36, 44, 62
hot sauce 29, 48
hulled 24

I
icing sugar 26
Italian seasoning 23

J
julienned 17

K
kalamata olives 14
Kalamata olives 10
kale 48, 51, 54
ketchup 30
kidney beans 59
king oyster mushrooms 10
kosher salt 11, 30, 55
Kosher salt 44, 60

L
lean ground beef 37
lean ground pork 39, 52
lean pork 36
lean pork tenderloin 36
leaves 25
lemon 41, 47, 49, 55, 63
lemongrass 10
lemon juice 17, 26, 32, 39, 44, 47, 48, 53, 58, 60, 65, 67, 70
Lemon juice 28
lemons 45
lemon zest 10, 14, 17, 46
light brown sugar 36, 69
light soy sauce 16, 36, 49
lime juice 31, 44, 52, 53
Lime wedges 31
liquid smoke 39
liquid stevia 42, 62, 63
liquid sweetener 14, 49
loaf stale ciabatta bread 68
low-fat buttermilk 29
low-fat unsweetened milk 67
low-sodium chicken broth 30, 32
low-sodium mustard 39
low-sodium soy sauce 28, 36
low-sodium tomato paste 44
lukewarm water 24
lump crabmeat 47

M
maple sauce 13
Maple syrup 13
marinated artichoke hearts 58
mashed potatoes 29

mayonnaise 24, 38, 53
medium shrimp 47
medjool dates 54
melted 10, 22, 23, 25
melted butter 66
melted coconut oil 66
mild hot sauce 11
mild red chili powder 31
milk 12, 13, 14, 23, 31, 41, 62, 67
minced 11, 13, 16, 19, 26, 28, 30
minced fresh parsley 38, 53
minced fresh rosemary 29, 53
minced fresh sage 29
minced fresh thyme 53
minced garlic 25, 31, 36, 44, 51, 61
minced ginger 61
misting 26
mixed salad leaves 39
mixed spice 14, 63
mozzarella cheese 15, 21, 34, 56, 62
Mozzarella cheese 40
mushroom-chicken cream soup 28
mushrooms 34
mustard 48

N
Nonstick Spray Oil 13
nutritional yeast 60
nutritional yeast flakes 51

O
old bay seasoning 46
Old Bay seasoning 47
olive oi 37
olive oil 10, 11, 14, 15, 17, 21, 22, 23, 24, 28, 30, 31, 32, 33, 34, 36, 37, 38, 40, 41, 42, 44, 46, 47, 49, 51, 53, 54, 55, 59, 60, 62
Olive oil 62
Olive oil spray 11, 46
onion 10, 11, 14, 16, 28, 30, 40, 41, 51, 60
onion powder 39, 41, 52, 56
onion rounds to garnish 31
orange jam 48, 65
oregano 33, 59
oyster sauce 37, 42

P
panko breadcrumbs 44, 46, 53, 54
paprika 15, 17, 25, 29, 32, 39, 45, 47, 56
Parmesan 30
Parmesan cheese 10, 11, 13, 14, 29, 32, 41, 46, 48, 52, 53, 55, 58
Parmigiano-Reggiano cheese 10
parsley 17, 41, 60
parsley leaves 17
part-skim ricotta cheese 65
pastry sheets 67
peaches 65
peanuts 17
peas 28
pecan halves 13
pecans 48
Pecorino Romano 30
peeled 14, 19, 44
peeled into ribbons 26
pepper 13, 14, 15, 16, 17, 21, 22, 28, 33, 34, 38, 41, 60, 62
Pepper 44, 56
Pepper Jack cheese 47
pesto 37
pesto with basil 56
pickled jalapeño 47
pine nuts 41
pitted 10, 14, 26
pitted dates 66
pizza dough 33
plain flour 46, 60
pomegranate seeds 62
pork 39
pork fillets 40
pork ribs 42

pork rinds 12, 15
pork tenderloin 36
potatoes 10, 17, 60
Powdered sugar 68
powdered sweetener 66, 69
preferably hard 13
pumpkin puree 22
pumpkin seeds 21
Pumpkin spice 21
pure maple syrup 68
pure vanilla extract 65, 68

Q
quartered 19
quick-cooking oats 68
quick oats 68

R
raisins 67
ranch dressing 56
Ranch dressing 33
ranch dressing mix 55
ranch seasoning mix 51
raw cashews 54
red bell pepper 31, 58
red cabbage 11
red hot sauce 33
red onion 14, 31, 58, 62
red pepper 14, 22
red pepper flakes 10, 19, 36, 47, 53, 60
reduced-fat cream cheese 61
reduced-fat Parmesan cheese 61
rice 40
rice vinegar 17, 28, 36
ricotta cheese 37
rinsed 14, 16, 26
ripe avocados 53
ripe bananas 26
roasted garlic 47
roasted red bell pepper 19
rolled oats 21
roma tomato 19
round steak 37

S
salmon fillet 46
salmon fillets 44, 46, 49
salsa 49
salt 10, 12, 13, 15, 16, 17, 20, 21, 22, 23, 24, 25, 29, 30, 31, 32, 38, 39, 41, 45, 48, 52, 53, 54, 55, 59, 60, 61, 62, 63, 65, 66, 67, 68, 69, 70
Salt 13, 14, 15, 16, 23, 28, 32, 33, 34, 36, 38, 40, 41, 44, 46, 48, 49, 58, 62
salted butter 23, 47
sausage 21
sausage meat 21
sausages 24
scallions 63
Scallions 44
scrambled 21
sea salt 10, 14, 19, 26, 37, 45, 54, 55, 58, 62
Sea salt 10, 41, 51
Seasoned salt 33
self raising flour 70
semi-dried tomatoes 41
semi-skimmed milk 22, 68
separate into rings 12
Serrano chilli 44
Serrano ham 39, 40
sesame oil 16, 28, 37, 42
sesame seeds 32, 34, 45
shallot 19, 29
shallot powder 47, 60
shaved 10, 14
sherry 37, 42
shredded 11, 15, 19, 25

shredded coconut 20, 24, 65
shredded cooked turkey 33
shredded low-sodium cheddar cheese 19
shredded red cabbage 39
shrimp 48
sifted 25
skinless, boneless chicken breast 32
sliced 16, 19, 20, 26
sliced almonds 55
sliced finely 25
sliced French onions 28
slice of ginger 42
slices tomatoes 24
slivered almonds 45
snow peas 38
soaked 16
soaked flaxseed 54
softened 10, 23
softened butter 10, 56
sour cream 10, 29, 38, 47, 65, 70
soured cream 28
soy sauce 32, 34, 37, 38, 40, 42, 61
spinach 60
spiralized 14, 26
sprigs fresh rosemary 28
spring onion 47, 51, 55
spring onions 56, 62
squeezed dry 37
squirty cream 70
sriracha chili sauce 53
sriracha sauce 17, 59
stalks 28
stevia 20, 22, 24
stone-ground cornmeal 29
strawberries 24
strawberry jam 70
sugar 13, 31, 37, 68
sugar-free maple syrup 16, 23, 25, 66
sugar-free syrup 48
Sugar to sprinkle 13
sultanas 68
sun-dried tomatoes 30, 32, 40
sunflower kernels 60
sunflower oil 63
sunflower seeds 55
sweet Marsala wine 30
sweet potato 17, 55
sweet potatoes 14, 19
Swiss chard 11
Swiss cheese 10, 11, 29

T
tahini 26
tarragon 38
teaspoon caster sugar 40
tempura butter 49
tenderloin steaks 40
thawed 22, 37
thinly sliced 10, 28
thinly sliced zucchini 51
thyme 33
toasted sesame oil 36, 61
tomato 25, 34, 58
tomatoes 15, 17, 34, 39
tomatoes with no salt 59
tomato ketchup 63
tomato paste 51
tomato sauce 33, 41
torn into pieces 11
turkey breast 31, 34
turmeric 16, 32, 61

U
uncooked brown rice 58
uncooked shrimp 44

unflavored gelatin 66
unsalted butter 30, 56, 65, 66, 67, 68, 69
unsalted chickpeas 51
unsalted natural peanut butter 54
unsalted pumpkin seeds 65
unsalted slivered almonds 65
unsweetened almond milk 19, 25, 60, 69
unsweetened cocoa powder 66, 69
unsweetened coconut 46
unsweetened coconut flakes 44
unsweetened shredded coconut 48, 67
unsweetened vanilla extract 65, 67
untoasted buckwheat flour 20

V
vanilla extract 12, 13, 20, 22, 24, 66, 68, 69
vegan butter 59
vegetable broth 58
vegetable oil 28, 31, 41
Vegetable oil 46
vegetable stock 55
vinegar 63

W
walnuts 16, 46, 63
warmed slightly 25
water 11, 12, 16, 23, 25, 29, 31, 36, 38, 42, 44, 49, 51, 60, 63, 67, 69
Water 10, 55
wheat germ 51
whipping cream 12
whisked 25
white balsamic vinegar 48
white bread 13
white bread flour 24
white button or cremini (baby Bella) mushrooms 30
white cabbage 40
white chocolate 68
white chocolate chunks 68
white mushrooms 38
white onion 42, 61
whites 22
white vinegar 33
white wine 58
whole chicken 28
wholemeal breadcrumbs 52
wholemeal burger buns 39
wholemeal flour 25
wholemeal toast 24
whole milk 70
whole plum 58
whole-wheat bread crumbs 11
wholewheat breadcrumbs 44
whole wheat flour 22, 30
whole-wheat flour 23
wild salmon 45
wonton wrappers 38
Wooden skewers 34
Worcestershire sauce 33

X
xanthan gum 47

Y
yellow onion 22, 23, 25, 36, 38, 59
yellow onions 11
yellow summer squash 53
yogurt 62

Z
zucchini 19, 25, 26, 62

Printed in Great Britain
by Amazon